Dance
was her
Religion

Dance Was Her Religion

The Sacred Choreography of

Isadora Duncan, Ruth St. Denis,

and Martha Graham

JANET LYNN ROSEMAN, PH.D.

FOREWORD BY ALONZO KING

Hohm Press
Prescott, Arizona

Cover design: Kim Johansen
Cover: Isadora Duncan Study by Abraham Walkowitz. Pastel on red paper. n.d. (ca. 1917)
Courtesy of University Gallery, University of Delaware. Gift of Virginia Zabriskie.
Layout and design: Tori Bushert

Library of Congress Cataloging-in-Publication Data

Roseman, Janet Lynn.
     Dance was her religion : the sacred choreography of Isadora Duncan, Ruth St. Denis and Martha Graham / Janet Lynn Roseman ; foreword by Alonzo King.
          p. cm.
     Includes bibliographical references and index.
     ISBN 1-890772-38-0 (pbk. : alk. paper)
1. Modern dance--History. 2. Dance--Religious aspects. 3. Duncan, Isadora, 1877-1927. 4. St. Denis, Ruth, 1880-1968. 5. Graham, Martha. I. Title.
     GV1783.R67 2004
     792.8'028'0922--dc22

                                        2004004444

HOHM PRESS
P.O. Box 2501
Prescott, AZ 86302
800-381-2700
http://www.hohmpress.com

This book was printed in the U.S.A. on acid-free
paper using soy ink.

08 07 06 05 04   5 4 3 2 1

For Mother Mary
and in tribute to the courageous lives of Isadora Duncan,
Ruth St. Denis, and Martha Graham who continue to inspire me.
"Sans Limites."

"The new humanity will be universal, and it will have the artist's attitude; that is, it will recognize that the immense value and beauty of the human being lies precisely in the fact that (s)he belongs to the two kingdoms of nature and spirit."

– Thomas Mann

Acknowledgements

To Dr. Sherry Eve Penn, my kind and loving friend and mentor who inspired this work when I was a Ph.D. candidate.

To Regina Sara Ryan, my editor at Hohm Press, who took on this project with enthusiasm and trust, and made this publishing experience a rich and sacred process.

To Alonzo King, whose friendship means the world to me, and whose generosity and talent know no earthly bounds.

To my mother, my favorite research companion, who helped me enormously in navigating the libraries in New York and Harvard. I would be lost without you.

To dad for his infinite patience and his financial support.

Blessings to the many people who kindly offered their art work and permissions for this book including: Janet Gardner Broske, Thomas Lisanti, Phil Karg, Norton Owen, Adrian Ravarour, Wendy Uyeda, Ronald Hussey, Jane Grossenbacher, Scott Hess, Kelly Borsheim, Kim Goldfarb, Mark Roseman, Lori Belilove, Meg Brooker, Iris J. Stewart, Sara Silver, Susan Brender, David Fullard, Pam Hagen, Timothy Eaton, Kabira Kirby, and Margaretta Mitchell.

Contents

Foreword

The physical body is a secretly coded condensation of limitless power encapsulated in form, and with its brain and spinal centers, it is a key that can open doors into the universal rhythms and Cause of all things. The ancient rishis of India knew the body as an externalization of metaphysical truth. Through their relentless investigations into the hidden potentialities within the body, they discovered the science of yoga, the foolproof way to reunite with our Origin.

Graham, Duncan, and St. Denis also understood our physical form as something sacred. They recognized it as a temple, divine symbol, and a center for receiving information and communicating ideas. These three women knew it was an instrument worthy of the deepest investigations, and they gave their lives to that undertaking. These trailblazers were in agreement with the Western medieval and ancient Eastern traditions that human beings are spirit housed in bodily vehicles. In the hierarchy of that physical domain, mind is above body, and spirit is above mind.

At a time when women's bodies where thought of as adjuncts to men's, St. Denis, Duncan, and Graham saw theirs as divine forms, which they relentlessly explored, to unearth and decipher new truths. They were listening to the pulse, breath, rhythm, and blood flow, of their physical instruments as a key into what was behind and beyond form. As the macrocosm is contained in the microcosm so the search and answer for all queries are found within.

Continuous concentrated inquiry into any realm can produce experiences of a knowing that the entire world may oppose with its logic and facts. This indisputable knowing, which comes from direct experience, is often a knowledge that science later confirms. There is no learning that can replace direct experience. Placing yourself in a physical shape and holding it for a length of time will inevitably produce a concomitant psychological state. Direct Experience needs no validation. You know because you have lived it. No matter how suppressed by weighty dogma, or entrenched custom, eternal truths always resurface.

The de-natured affectations that had infected classical ballet at the time where abhorrent to these truth seekers. Their efforts at authenticity created a new sky brought by the debris clearing wind of honesty.

In every evolutionary cycle there is a period of darkness. A time when education suffocates individuality and questioning. Obscurity prevails, form is idolized, energy is externalized and out of rhythm. Nothing is questioned. And consistently during these times there are remarkable people who against the grain of trend and popular opinion listen to themselves. The inner voice is so persistent that it has to have its say regardless of consequence. Janet Lynn Roseman has chosen to speak on three such heroines who were leaders in a time when women were to be appreciated for how they looked and behaved, and the body was thought of primarily as a source of pleasure or something vulgar that should be hidden. As the mathematical precision of the skies informed ancient astronomers about the precession of the equinox so these earthly bodies informed these three women about movement and the essential nature of things.

– Alonzo King
Choreographer and Artistic Director,
Alonzo King's LINES Ballet; linesballet.org
March 2004

Isadora Duncan Study by Abraham Walkowitz. Pastel on black paper. n.d. (ca. 1917) Courtesy of University Gallery, University of Delaware. Gift of Virginia Zabriskie.

Young Isadora Duncan removed her heavy shoes and clothes, which felt like her prison, and danced naked by the sea. "And it seemed to me as if the sea and all the trees were dancing with me," she wrote in her autobiography many years later.[1]

Across the country, eleven-year-old Ruth St. Denis read the New Testament to herself in her room. Attempting to recreate the biblical clothing and sacred dances of the past, she dressed up in bath towels and wooden sandals, fastening a large cord at her waist. Staring intently in her bedroom mirror she slowly moved her body in solemn ritual. She would repeat these holy ceremonies again and again during her lifetime in sacred dance.

And, in the quiet and somber atmosphere of a Presbyterian church in Pittsburgh, a two-year-old Martha Graham joyfully lifted her skirts and danced her way down the center aisle of the chapel, as her horrified family looked on.

Deeply embedded in the youthful bodies of Isadora Duncan, Ruth St. Denis and Martha Graham was an intuitive understanding of the sacred and liberating aspects of the dance. Enduring beyond the childish glee of movement, these three pioneers of dance recognized that the truths, miracles, revelations and splendors of the human form would be their life's work. They not only revolutionized the dance form, but also succeeded in resurrecting the tenet that movement was a sacred and ecstatic experience.

Children inherently know the ecstasy and the boundless feeling that movement can provide. Their primal and basic need for motion is not self-conscious or planned, but directly experienced in the body. Remember when you used to sway higher and higher on a backyard swing – attempting to literally swing into the blue sky? Or when you played the game Statues with friends who propelled your body into magical forms? These childhood games offered a chance to embody freedom, a freedom that is both in and of the body.

Unfortunately, the liberating experiences of movement that we have as children are quickly forgotten as we mature. We soon adopt "acceptable" patterns of motion to blend in with our world – a world that frequently asks us to shut down our sacred impulses, to breathe shallowly, to hold our bodies tightly. These bodily restrictions continue as we become more and more removed from the spontaneous ecstasy that we held inside when we were young. Forgotten is the truth that to be lost in motion is part of our birthright.

Dance has always contained these holy opportunities to re-align our bodies with our spiritual longings. And, those longings are the real reason that most people choose to dance.

Joan Dexter Blackmer, a Jungian psychologist and a modern dancer, wrote what I consider to be one of the best descriptions as to why I (and others) am drawn to the dance. "Behind the effort needed to become a dancer, as I see it, lies a deep urge to be allowed into sacred time and space, to open the earthly body and what it can communicate to an other-worldly energy. The dance itself becomes, for a moment, the vessel into which sacred energies may flow, a vehicle for manifestation of the gods. No experience is as fully alive as having that god-like energy move through one."[2] Dancing provides the dancer an opportunity to align through movement with the life force of the body, another important aspect of the truth about why we dance. "Difficult but not impossible, is the understanding that every one of us carries within him[her] a secret temple and that is from there only that [s]he must find an artistic expression of the holy purpose of movement."[3]

The inherent powers of dance are so pure and so strong that they often stay inside of us long after the "movement" experience has ended. This transformation can occur in the kinesthetic messages that the body is able to intuit and to understand. Rudolf Steiner, a prolific Austrian philosopher and visionary, developed his ideas for eurythmy – a psycho-spiritual movement technique – as a sacred dance form that could align the body with the spirit through movement and speech. He considered dance "a gift of the gods" and a potent expression of the spiritual worlds on earth. Steiner also believed that the dancer had a responsibility and an obligation to act as a conduit between the worlds of spirit and matter.

This responsibility was readily apparent to Isadora Duncan, Ruth St. Denis and Martha Graham. They knew that dance was not only their religion, but it was their personal connection between those two worlds. Unencumbered with the conventional beliefs of their time, they adhered to their own internal laws. Enduring ridicule, humiliation, mean-spirited reviews, betrayals, censorship and financial struggles, they were willing to pay a price for their singular philosophies. Unafraid to celebrate the power of the female body, each of these blessed women remained true to herself, without abandoning her visions for popularity's sake.

Their beliefs about the power and sanctity of the human form in dance was an extraordinary concept that posed a harsh contrast to the theatrical dances being performed on the stage during that era. The stigma of choosing a career as a dancer was ever present, even though the suffragette movement was coming into its own in the early 1920s. Many still held that dancers were "loose women," void of morals and virtue. Appalled by such stereotypes, Isadora Duncan, Ruth St. Denis and Martha Graham changed the artistic landscape of dance by reclaiming the heart of dance, alchemically altering its form from the frivolity of vaudeville to the holy. Establishing schools, performing across the globe, and speaking articulately about the healing and sacred powers of dance, they elevated the dance form forever.

Isadora Duncan was not afraid to combat her critics even when publicly humiliated in the press or prevented from presenting her concerts in the United States. Clad in her signature free-flowing tunic, both on-stage and off, in 1922, while promoting a series of concerts in Boston, she told a reporter, "If my art is symbolic, it is symbolic of the freedom of women." A feminist before the word was coined, Duncan believed that the fashions of the day were suffocating for women. She refused to wear corsets, tight layers of clothing and shoes, since such clothing prohibited women from experiencing their natural female forms. Accused by the mayor of Boston for indecent exposure, her concerts in that city were promptly canceled. Although she was aware of her critics, she didn't let outside attempts of controlling her art stop her. When she was on tour in Indianapolis (in the same year that her concerts were banned in Massachusetts), Duncan was forced to perform while members of the police department waited in the wings, scrutinizing her every move, eager to arrest her if the tunic she was wearing revealed any part of her body. The pastors of the Methodist Episcopal Church in St. Louis condemned her performances as "the grossest violation of the properties of life," and denounced her as being "a menace to the nation."[4]

Condemnation and accusations were also common during Ruth St. Denis's life. She dared to present sacred dances on the stage, embodying the figures of goddesses from ancient cultures, and her reviewers were not always welcoming. After watching her performance as an Indian goddess, clad only in ceremonial dress, one audience member declared that she was "indecent." Even the dance reviewer from the *New York Telegraph* wrote that "her dances were nothing more or less than a mixture of hoochee-koochee and cake walk."[5] Attempting to align the dance with the godhead, St. Denis spent much of her latter life dancing in churches and for her efforts, she frequently received hate-mail accusing her of "attacking the purity of the church."

In the early days of Martha Graham's career, she was urged to stop performing. When a friend attended one of her performances, she told Martha that her work was "simply dreadful." When asked how long she intended to keep this up, Graham replied, "As long as I've got an audience."

Isadora Duncan, Ruth St. Denis, and Martha Graham considered themselves prophets of dance. Allowing spiritual energies to fill them, the dance was their prayer and their bodies were their texts. Unlike traditional clergy, they didn't need a church preferring to create sacred temples of learning in which they could teach their students how to discover their own holy doctrines. In their respective schools, they succeeded in not only elevating the very technique and form of dance from its standard and stilted vocabulary, but created new dance techniques – sacred techniques which have laid the groundwork for dance training today. Establishing these new sacred vistas for dancers, each of these women provided a lush philosophical foundation about how the powers of movement could transform not only the consciousness of the dancers performing, but also the consciousness of their audiences. They actually brought the elements of the divine onto the stage. In their schools, they espoused a holy, even mystical, training to dancers, not only enabling them to bring these sanctified aspects of dance to the public, but providing them with the opportunity to learn a body-based spirituality.

Tragically, many dance scholars and academics are dismissive of their accomplishments, often trivializing their works, failing to realize that these women were much more than brilliant dancers and choreographers, they were seminal spiritual thinkers. In the chapters that follow, their breath of vision, accomplishments, and philosophies will be discussed at length.

Isadora Duncan, Ruth St. Denis and Martha Graham were articulate and insightful spokespersons for the art of dance, integrating their discoveries of the natural and supernatural worlds. Writing voluminously about the sacred nature of the body, their published and unpublished articles, interviews, and taped conversations assert their keen insights. The fact that all three women created their own schools of training, successfully performed around the world, and ran their own businesses tells us much about their perseverance in a man's domain. Each of left the world an enormous artistic and philosophical legacy.

The Sacred Dance

Sacred choreography has been a natural expression of human beings in all civilizations, cultures and religions. Not merely an adjunct to worship, it was integral to all worship. The earliest of all art forms, dance has endured since humankind inhabited the earth. Dance has been allied with religious and spiritual experiences since primitive humans danced in rituals to please and placate their gods. It has always been sacred self-expression, and even a mystical experience when, in pure form, dancing united the body both physically and devotionally. As dance evolved, the practice and training of dancers for performance became the norm, thus moving its focus from inside to outside the dancer. God or spirit was forgotten after the mystical elements were replaced and the attention to the sacred was abandoned.

Historically, the body has always conveyed the sacred symbology of the universe and of the gods. In fact, the ancient name for "history" comes from *histor*, meaning "a dancer." This word was also the root for other derivatives including *minister* (*Min-Istria*.)[6] This parallel between "dance" and "minister" takes on new meaning when you consider that during the earliest part of the nineteenth century, dance consisted of "entertainment" in vaudeville programs, losing its holy intent. It is more of a wonder that Duncan, St. Denis, and Graham chose to create sacred choreography on the stage, not merely as performance, but as sacred revelations for their audiences. They challenged both audiences and critics to experience dance as a sacred art form. This was an ancient idea, yet revolutionary.

Following in the tradition of the mystics, these three women were seeking alignment with divine forces to achieve both ecstasy and enlightenment. Implicit in the creation of sacred choreographies was the potential to enter into an ecstatic and mystical state. Graham's notebooks testify to that. "What are the techniques of ecstasy," she asks. "Prayer — union with the gods."[7]

Spiritual vitality is alive in the soul in the same way as the marrow of the hips in the flesh.
– Hildegard of Bingen, German prophet and mystic.

During the fifth century AD, the philosopher Proclus argued that "contemplative thought" a vehicle for achieving union with God, was not in itself sufficient for enlightenment. It had to be coupled with theurgy, or the ritual contacting of the god by allowing that particular god to possess one's body during the ritual.[8] Theurgy is the real reason why so many people throughout the centuries were and are drawn to the dance. We need only pay attention to the effect that dance has upon us to understand the link between body and spirit. When we dance, we feel good. We may feel connected to spirit and open to a greater energetic presence. Duncan, St. Denis, and Graham were well versed in these divine energies. I believe that movement can provide access to these otherworldly moments.

Dance for the Goddess

The volume of works that Isadora, Ruth, and Martha created in their lifetimes is staggering, and each of their dances contains a sacred theme. Duncan's *Ave Maria*, considered one of her best works, was made when she was grieving the death of her children in a tragic automobile accident. On-stage, Duncan transmuted her grief into an intimate spiritual encounter, personally identifying with the Virgin Mary, who like her, had lost her beloved child. Her connection with the Virgin Mary, an archetype of the goddess, was apt not only for her personal consolation, but because she believed that through her dancing she offered her audiences the opportunity to see spiritual forces activated through her own body.

St. Denis chose to create numerous concerts in which she became the goddess. Using her body as "an instrument of spiritual revelation," she untiringly researched each of her goddess figures in architectural, metaphysical and historical books, much like an actress might, but there was a profound difference; the actress would study the research to present the character on-stage as realistically as possible, while St. Denis did not permit herself to act out a mental composition of a sacred figure from afar. Instead, she embodied that person, or sacred quality, and believed that the training in this embodiment was the essence of her work.[9] Ruth was one of the first artists to bring dancing into the sacred environment of a church thus inspiring the field of modern liturgical dance. As she matured, she changed her performance venues from the commercial to the holy.

Graham's fascination with the spiritual quest of the Divine Feminine is apparent in her works. She was devoted to Jungian philosophy, had a Jungian therapist, and that knowledge and consciousness had an important imprint in her dances. The archetypes of the "Divine Mother" and "Goddess" appear again and again in her choreographies with the central theme of the Divine Feminine.

*Ruth St. Denis as the Madonna. She would continue to portray the Virgin Mary
during her lifetime. Courtesy of Jacob's Pillow Photo Archive.*

St. Denis not only choreographed dances to many goddess figures, she created hundreds of programs, sometimes presented as full-scale pageants, honoring the Virgin Mary and Jesus. Her solo works included *The Blue Madonna*, *Masque of Mary*, and *The Gold Madonna*.

Steeped in metaphysical knowledge as well as theological understandings, St. Denis chose the Virgin Mary as her subject for a gorgeous book of poetry entitled, *Lotus Light*. Because she believed the Madonna to be the ultimate and most pure symbol of creation and compassion, St. Denis's words pay tribute to her.

> We are all Love beings
> Groping our blind way towards ecstasy.
> In the silent temple
> Of the Heart
> We lift imploring hands
> Waiting for the Divine annunciation.
> We are all Mary
> Waiting to conceive
> And bear the Christ Child.[10]

Graham's resonance with the Madonna in her first choreographed work, *A Florentine Madonna*, served as a foundation for countless other dances in her career that included the Virgin Mary as the pivotal female character. Her choreographic legacy contained images not only of the Virgin Mary, but of saints and angels. Even at age ninety-seven, she was working on her final piece called *Goddess*, which was never finished.

Personal Inspiration

I have long loved the Virgin Mary, and as her devotee I have studied her images in hundreds of churches across the country, photographing her, attempting to learn her secrets. I was drawn to the works and philosophies of Isadora Duncan, Ruth St. Denis and Martha Graham because I

The Virgin Mary with poinsettia.
Courtesy of photographer Scott Hess.

wanted to investigate the parallels between their devotion to the Virgin Mary and my own. Although, I am academically trained as a dance scholar and critic, I have always been drawn to the sacred, an area that is frequently excised from scholarly dance texts, yet abundant in religious texts. I couldn't find contemporary spiritual teachers, and I hoped that these three women could guide me in my own sacred quest. Why did they choose to dance — to embody the Virgin Mary? What was their relationship to her? Were they searching too?

As a professional dance critic, I loved to watch dancers who could illustrate much more than technical acumen or circus tricks. I wanted to experience dance performances as a revelation. I have tried, throughout my career, to write about dance from a sacred perspective, and many times, the mere mention of spirituality in dance has been edited out of my dance columns. When I have presented papers at academic conferences on the subject of dance and spirituality, often, the reactions from my academic peers have been hostile. Why was this spiritual realm so threatening I wondered.

I have experienced the alignment of body and spirit in my own dance practice and this connection to spirit, or allowing sacred energies to fill my body, has altered my life. This sense of heightened awareness is written about by many mystics and creative artists. I am aware of the flow of these energies when I dance, and it is not unusual for me to feel a band or flow of energies flowing from out of my hands when I am at the barre. I knew that many of the experiences of energy that I witnessed inside and outside my own body happened to other dancers, and I wanted to delve deeper to understand this mystical energy and the interaction between dance and metaphysical states.[11] Carl Jung believed that, "Our conscious idea of God is abstract and remote. One hardly dares to speak of it. It has become taboo, or it is such a worn-out coin that one can hardly exchange it."[12] I agree. These metaphysical states that are natural in movement are part of that taboo and I wanted to give voice to that understanding.

How did the influences of the Divine impact the creative choreographic works to the Virgin Mary of Isadora Duncan, Ruth St. Denis, and Martha Graham? This question haunted me while I was in graduate school studying for a Ph.D. in dance theory and criticism. I have always been called to the spiritual aspects of dance and the arts and I wanted to write a book, based on my research, which could rediscover and elevate the dance arts to what their original intention was; dance as a divine offering. I knew the choreographic works of these three women well, and was particularly struck by how often their philosophical contributions were ignored, and denigrated, particularly their spiritual philosophies. It disturbed me that these artists who possessed such rich, deep mystical understandings did not have their spiritual contributions cited alongside other spiritual philosophers. Countless books relate the life and contributions of Isadora Duncan, Ruth St. Denis, and Martha Graham, yet it is rare to find historical books that mention their spiritual achievements or probe their personal connections to the Virgin Mary and chronicle their sacred visions.

This book is written not only to honor the sacred roots of the dance, but to historically restore these three dance pioneers to their rightful places as spiritual philosophers. It is my wish that this book will give readers pause and an opportunity to reconsider not only the choreographic accomplishments of these artists, but insight into their connections to the Divine. This is a book for dancers, dance lovers, spiritual seekers, historians, and those in search of illumination.

I am inspired that spirituality is addressed more and more in the mass media. Bookstores are laden with novels and trade paperbacks about the Virgin Mary and other biblical figures, subjects that previously had no appeal for a secular audience. This yearning for the knowledge of the sacred, not only provides a soothing balm, but also is indicative of a spiritual vacuum that many people experience. In a world filled with economic uncertainty, political upheaval across the globe, ecological destruction, and a loss of sacred consciousness in everyday human interactions, the spiritual philosophies of Isadora Duncan, Ruth St. Denis and Martha Graham can teach us new ways to be in the world. During times of turmoil, their body-centered mysticism speaks volumes about achieving balance, stillness, and clarity. Their deeply studied knowledge about the essential wisdom of the body and visions for a sacred world has much to offer, even many years after their deaths. Isadora Duncan wrote that: "The dance is not only the art that gives free expression to the human soul through movement, but also the foundation of a complete conception of life, more free, more harmonious, more natural."[13]

May you find that freedom in your own life.

Isadora Duncan Study by Abraham Walkowitz. Pen and ink. n.d. (ca. 1915-1920.)
Courtesy of University Gallery, University of Delaware. Gift of Virginia Zabriskie.

Chapter 1

Dancing for God

I am hard-pressed to name a pre-Christian culture that did not dance, for dance was the pre-dominant medium of expression to invoke the gods, to grant blessings for the community, to insure that the crops would be plentiful, and to integrate members of the community in sacred form. Considered the oldest of arts, the mythological origins of dance are attributed to Terpischore, the muse of dance, who continues to inspire dancers of today. Before ballet, modern dance, tap, or any other form, dance was religious ritual. People of all shapes, sizes, and ethnic origin would gather to honor their gods and goddesses through animal dances, circle dances, ecstatic dances, healing dances, and other ritualistic ceremonies.

Dance honors the sacredness of life and death, and prehistoric humans painted their dances upon the walls of their caves. Historically, this ancestral rite for connection to the deities has taken a wide variety of forms, including the mystical spinning of the whirling dervishes of Turkey and the Middle East, African ceremonial dances, and Native American rituals. The fundamental call for dance as a form of worship is that it can provide an opportunity for embodying exalted states; and this opportunity is the indisputable reason that humans – from the past through modern times – dance.

Dance and religion have been strange bedfellows, sometimes welcome, more often not. The Bible has numerous words to describe dancing: *hägag* (to dance in a circle), *säbab* (encircle), *rägad* and *pizzëz* (to skip), *gippës* and *dillëg* (to jump), *kirkër* (to whirl or pirouette), *päsah* (the limping dance), *hyl/hll* (perform a whirling dance), *sihëq* (to dance or play).[1] What is disturbing about the absence of dance as an acceptable form of worship within Christianity through the ages is the fact that Jesus danced. The Acts of St. John in the Apocrypha describe Jesus's "Round Dance" at length. Apparently it took place after the Last Supper with Jesus dancing in the middle of the circle surrounded by his followers, who danced around him while he recited the following hymn:

PRAISE to thee, Logos!
Praise to thee, Logos! Praise to thee, Grace, Amen.
I will be saved and I shall save. Amen.
I will be delivered and I shall deliver. Amen.
Grace dances in the round-dance.
I will play upon the flute, let all dance. Amen.
The twelve on high dance their ring-dance. Amen.
It is the duty of all to dance on high. Amen.
Who dances not, knows not what will happen. Amen.
And, if you take part in my straight dance behold
yourself in Me, the Speaker, and when you behold
what I do then do not disclose my mysteries. When
you dance, think what I do: that is your suffering, the
suffering of mankind, which I wish to suffer. I dance,
but you must think of the whole and when you have
thought then say, Praise to the Father.[2]

The Greek writer Lucian wrote during the second century AD that "one cannot find a single mystery induction not associated with the dance."[3] This is a powerful sentence when one considers that most often dances to the Virgin Mary and to the gods were often parallel with the sacred mysteries of the universe.

Before the birth of Jesus, "mystery schools" trained initiates in metaphysics, healing, and alchemy. These students were considered priests or priestesses, and they used their bodies in dance and movement in order to communicate with spirit. Preserved in esoteric mystery schools, the teachings and dances had one key objective – communion and union with the Godhead. This concept of merging the ecstatic through movement reached across the barriers of time into the minds of Isadora Duncan, Ruth St. Denis, and Martha Graham who resurrected the eternal presence of the Divine Feminine.

In our day, Carla de Sola, a prominent figure in contemporary liturgical dance, has created many dances in honor of God and the Virgin Mary. One of her most powerful pieces merges the words of the Rosary prayer with movement. Presenting sacred dance in churches across the country, de Sola's work has contributed greatly to the re-discovery of dance as sacred form. Alonzo King, the artistic director for LINES Ballet in San Francisco, is another contemporary choreographer who works within the holy realm. His choreography turns the theatre into a sanctuary, echoing dance's earliest intention. One cannot dismiss the sacred elements of his work and his ceaseless exploration for the divine in dance. Unlike most dance companies that are more concerned with offering gymnastic feats on stage, King recognizes that the purpose of dance is transformative. "The artist/dancer is not an exhibitionist or looking to display his or her personality. The dancers first and primary duty is to radiate, like the sun. To work is to do something; to serve is to become something. Ideally, the dancer really wants to be danced, rather than to dance. Dancing is about Spirit."[4]

Ring Dances

Most religious sects possess the image of the circle for some aspect of their religious rites, since the circle is a sacred geometrical form. Universally accepted as the symbol of eternity and never-ending existence, it is also the monogram of God (or Goddess), and represents the perfection of the everlasting God. The circle is also an illustration of the celestial skies above us, mirroring the harmony of the east, west, north, and south, as well as the ethereal realms. Linked to the mysteries of the cosmos, dancers would gather together in circular formation to pay homage to their deities, and ask for blessings.

Examining the dances of ancient Crete offers important insights as to how they were performed. The poet Sappho wrote: "Thus, once upon a time the Cretan woman danced rhythmically with delicate feet around a beautiful altar, treading upon the soft, smooth flowers of the meadow."[5] It is highly likely that the dances and hymns that were later performed in honor of the Virgin Mary had their roots in

"Encircling is the incorporating, the giving and receiving of power. While it encloses and possesses, the circle also empowers through a concentration of energy that is ever-flowing and ever-changing. The circle leads back into itself and so is symbol of unity, the Absolute, perfection." – Iris Stewart, SWSD, 149.

these early dances because circle dances, and "especially those with hands clasped, have, for all their simplicity, a highly mystical significance among all ancient peoples. The Cretans in particular believed that their great goddess could be induced by prayer, offerings and a ceremonial dance to appear to them. This dance then, becomes an invocation dance in which women dancers moved in an open circle, with arms upraised. There is also evidence that is some cases, dancers, relaxed in a circular formation, formed patterns or designs, and then stood still, so that the goddess and spectators might see them."[6]

During the twelfth century, Honorus, a Christian philosopher, paid homage to the significance of these dances and his description provides valuable historical information.

> [In the] origin in the ring-dance of antiquity before the false gods, ensnared by their delusions, both praised their gods with their voices and served them with their bodies. But, in their ring-dances…in the clasping of their hands, the union of the elements; in the sounds of the song the harmony of the planets; in the gestures of the body the movements of the celestial bodies; in the clapping of the hands and the stamping of the feet the sound of thunder; something which the faithful, converting all to the true service of God. They danced ring-dances.[7]

A variation on circle dances is the rite of circumambulation. Participants walked around a circular path or labyrinth that surrounded a sacred site.

> The classic labyrinth is a single path meant for meditative circumambulation. It was originally a spiral, but slowly evolved into the maze of angular turns familiar to us today. In the ancient world, prayer was an active, trance-inducing combination of chanting, music and dance, and it is most likely that initiates

*In this painting at the cathedral in Pienza, Italy, real women,
not angels, circle the Virgin Mary and dance.
Courtesy of Iris J. Stewart and photographer Sara Silver.*

danced the sacred spiral [of the labyrinth]. The danced line into the labyrinth was a sacred path into the inner ream of the goddess.[8]

Modern day pilgrims have adapted this ceremony, and the popularity of labyrinths, particularly in church settings, reflects its ancient tradition. In 341 AD, the bishop of Milan encouraged his congregates to participate in sacred dancing because he believed that the circle dance in particular offered access to the mystical dimension and was a form of adoration to God.

> The Lord bids us to dance, not merely with circling movements of the body, but with pious faith in him. For just as [s]he who dances with the body at one time floats ecstatically, at another leaps in the air and at another by varying dances pays reverence, so also [s]he who dances in the spirit with a burning faith is carried aloft, is uplifted to the stars, and at the same time solemnly glorifies Heaven by the dances of the thought of Paradise. And just as [s]he who dances with the body rushing the rotating movements of the limbs, acquires the right to share in the round dance – in the same way [s]he who dances the spiritual dance, always moving in the ecstasy of faith, acquires the right to dance in the ring of all creation.[9]

This mystical and spiritual connection is central to the idea of the ring-dance. The use of the circle as a sacred dance form is as old as humanity itself. Mimicking the sun, the stars and the moon in the heavens, the circle is a symbol of consciousness. The great psychiatrist Carl Jung, no stranger to mystical philosophy, therapeutically utilized the drawing of the circle or mandala to help his patients uncover and reveal the inner reflection of their personalities. Native Americans employ the circle in sacred dance ceremonies since it is a universal and concrete manifestation for unity and wholeness.

By synchronizing one's actions with the Divine plan, it is thought that goodness will result. It is for this reason that contact with the sacred realities defined by the circle is thought to be healing.[10]

Dance Madness

Until the fifth century of the Christian era, dance was considered a natural vehicle for expressing the joys of faith and devotion, and it wasn't until the Middle Ages that the integration of dance and religion began to be regulated by church authorities. Solo dancing and dancing between the sexes was strictly off-limits. Sacred choreography was encouraged during religious holidays and special services, but the warnings of St. Augustine, as early as 394 AD, against "frivolous or unseemly dancing," were probably repeated to condemn the choreomaniacs of the Middle Ages All night and day on the streets and in the churches of Germany, thousands of choreomaniacs danced until they collapsed from exhaustion. Their erratic movements and jumps into the air were an expression of their beliefs that if they allowed their feet to land on the ground, they would jump into pools of blood. Some of the dancers even proclaimed that they had visions of heaven during their ecstatic states.

Understandably, the choreomaniacs were considered by the clergy to be mad and possessed by the devil. Many of the dancers participated in exorcism rites, as the church insisted that "demons had overtaken their bodies." Other church authorities claimed that their illnesses stemmed from the fact that these choreomaniacs were illegitimate, and not properly baptized because their mothers were prostitutes.

Dancing in front of the altar of the Virgin Mary in the cathedral of Aachen, Germany, a description of their

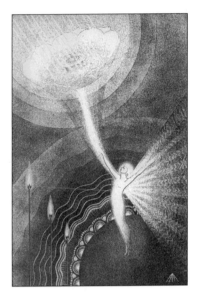

Artist Ruth Harwood captures the spiritual reflection of Ruth St. Denis's art. Courtesy of The Ruth Harwood Papers, Manuscripts Division, Marriott Library, University of Utah.

so-called possession by the devil, written many years later in 1403, is captivating, and creates a powerful visual image.

> This is how it happened; persons of both sexes, possessed by devils and half-naked set wreaths on their heads, and began their dances and not only in market places, but in churches. They were free of all modesty and in their songs, they uttered the names of devils never before heard. When the dance was finished the demons would torment their breasts with dreadful pains till they raged and shouted that they would die unless something bound them tightly and firmly about the waist.[11]

During the same year of the dance epidemic at Aachen, a law was passed in this area (on November 18, 1374) proclaiming it illegal to dance in the streets or inside churches, but curiously, dancing was permitted in private homes. These epidemics harmed the integration of dance in a liturgical setting, a fear that has been passed on for generations. During the time of the Black Plague (1347-1373), the bubonic plague and pneumonia killed half of the entire population of Europe. "The Dance of Death," or *Dance Macabre*, was an implicit reaction to such human devastation. During the daily funeral processions, frenzied outbursts of dance called "danseomania" occurred. Were the dances of the Medieval period neurological disorders, as some physicians and scholars have thought, or simply outlets for emotional and physical release? Some scholars point to either or both causes. "During the 14th century plague epidemic in central Europe, Christians and pagans danced to seek protection from illness. These dances based on religious fervor, pagan tradition or superstition, may have led to epidemics of mass hysteria. Neurologists later surmised that these epidemics were outbreaks of a disorder known has hysteric chorea, which caused involuntary dance movement."[12]

Although dance was not entirely eradicated from church services during the late fourteenth century, the many edicts dictating how and when dance could be performed contributed to its demise, and the remnants of those edicts furthered the church's cause to banish sacred dance rituals.

The Meaning of Ritual

The real purpose behind the earliest forms of dance was not so much to appease the gods but to offer the opportunity for participants to be lost in the dance – to lose their boundaries while totally immersed in sacred states. Early dance rituals provided form, a container made of human flesh. Ritual, by definition, belongs neither to this world nor to the Divine, but "plays the role of the intermediary between the two for interpersonal centering and spiritual balancing. Dance as ritual has always been a way to honor the sacred, the mystery, the ever present flow of the Divine forces."[13] The momentous split that turned dance-worship in the devotional setting into entertainment was a split between the sacred and the profane. "Devotional dances gradually became commissioned works for the enjoyment of the ruling spectators for provocative entertainment. Dance was transformed from a religious act or ceremonial rite into a work of art intended for the observer and from these changes arose a culture of dance as theater and entertainment."[14]

Ruth St. Denis, who devoted her life to return dance to its rightful place as sacred encounter, declared, "Every time I danced before an audience, I wished to say through my body that man in all his arts and spiritual perception must be worshiping the godhead, whatever name it is called, Jehovah, Brahma, Allah. The few who perceived this only made me reach the farther to touch all those who came."[15]

Isadora Duncan, too, struggled to teach people about the sanctification of the body through the dance, a lesson that was not always well received. She asserted that "No one seems to understand, but I am trying to teach the world to think as

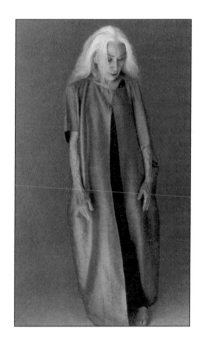

Legendary dancer Eleanor King in "Robe." Courtesy of photographer Jane Grossenbacher.

I do. I have the idea that I was born with, and my idea is the idea of life. My ideal would be to found a temple of the beautiful. I actively work to promote my idea of the reconstruction of the ancient dances, and the ancient dress."[16]

Ritual movement was, and still is, a part of a highly symbolic process by which one's life gained transcendent significance. This urging, this longing and expectant receivership for the dancers to merge with the divine energies in their bodies is apparent in all sacred dance ceremonies. The desire for unity and integration of the body with spirit answered the need for that communication. In the ritual itself, the participants were part of something larger than themselves, and each self was not important, but the whole of Selves was what mattered the most.

According to Jungian analyst Marion Woodman, a dancer herself, this understanding is part of our inner knowing. "Many of us in drought-stricken weeks have either danced our dance or understood in our bones what the dance is all about," she wrote. "The steady beat [of the movement of our bodies], activates our central nervous system that in turn releases the healing power of the instinctual unconscious."[17]

The idea of divine energies flowing through our bodies was well known to the mystics of every age, even though many mystics sought to remove themselves from their bodies in order to communicate with God. These divine energies were available to non-mystics as well. Martha Graham, when she was making the dance *Seraphic Dialogue*, spoke about invisible energies and voices she heard around her. She wrote in her autobiography, *Blood Memory*, "I have been aware of unseen things around me, a certain sense of that [energetic] movement. I don't know what to call them, sense beings perhaps, or spirits or a kind of energy that dominates. There's even a presence that I can feel walking through my home. I know that something exists there."[18]

While we commonly associate mystical understanding and revelation with the mind and heart, something achieved through prayer and contemplation, the body too can be a dynamic channel of spiritual insight – a vehicle of communion. In the tenth century, the Eastern Orthodox saint, Symeon, called "the New Theologian," wrote:

> We awaken in Christ's body
> as Christ awakens our bodies,
> and my poor hand is Christ. He enters
> my foot, and is infinitely me…
>
> For if we genuinely love him,
> we wake up inside Christ's body
>
> where all our body, all over,
> every most hidden part of it,
> is realized in joy as Him,
> and He makes us utterly real…
>
> and recognized as whole, lovely,
> and radiant in His light.[19]

Ruth St. Denis believed that she was in service to such a higher dimension when she danced, and the recurring themes of God/Goddess appear over and over again in her work. In 1925, she wrote a proclamation titled "I DEMAND OF THE DANCE," stating St. Symeon's prayer in her own words: "I demand of the dance – more than any of the other arts – that it reveal the God in humanity – not merely the scientific and beautiful forms that the body can be made to assume, but the very divine self."[20]

That dance could serve a ritual function of consecration before the throne of the Godhead was also apparent to the great choreographer George Balanchine. Often he spoke about this link to the spiritual worlds. "I got a message. Each one of us is here to serve on the earth. And probably I was sent here to see and hear – that's all I can do. I don't create or invent anything, I assemble. God already made everything."[21]

Isadora Duncan never doubted that her dance rituals/ceremonies upon the stage were sacred. "I sought the source of spiritual expression to flow into the channels of the body filling it with vibrating light – the centrifugal force reflecting the spirit's vision."[22]

The fourteenth-century mystic St. Teresa of Àvila understood the power of sacred movement. Embraced by the Divine in prayer, she wrote about her experiences with keen insight, and her words add momentum to the understanding of ritual dance as a spiritual experience.

> To return to this sudden rapture of the spirit. The soul really does seem to have left the body. The body is, however not lifeless, and, though clearly not dead, yet the person cannot tell whether her spirit remains within her body or not. *She feels wholly transported into another state very different from the one we live in.* There, an unearthly light is revealed which she could never have imagined had she spent her entire life trying to dream it up. In an instant her mind is alert to so much at once, that the intellect and imagination could never list a tiny part of it all, even if they had the time to do so…Just as the sun's rays seem to reach the earth the minute it shines in the sky, *so the soul and the spirit are one and the same thing…*And I can give no other name for this activity than "flight"…Great mysteries are revealed in this time. When the person returns to consciousness she is so enriched that she holds all the world's trappings as filth compared to what she has seen.[23]

In the italicized text, it is easy to compare what St. Teresa learned in her visions with the sacred encounters that Isadora Duncan, Ruth St. Denis and Martha Graham experienced. To be "fully transported into another state very different from the one we live in," is to be lost in the sacred dance. When "the soul and the spirit are one and the same thing," the body and the soul are united. We know that St. Teresa danced in the privacy of her own room, and we may imagine that those sacred dances might have become an integral part of her prayer ritual.

The Healing Aspects of Dance

Isadora Duncan, Ruth St. Denis and Martha Graham experienced ecstatic states when they danced, states that most probably activated their *chakras*, thus offering them the ability to receive spiritual energies that could propel them to a higher state of consciousness. "*Chakra*" is a Sanskrit word meaning "wheel of light." Residing in key points in the body, the chakras form a profound and intricate system of energy centers. These centers in the human body connect to transcendent forces of the spiritual universe.

Each of these women was a student of Eastern religion, and was well aware of the chakra system as a guide for learning more about higher dimensions. They used this knowledge not only for personal enlightenment, but also in their choreography and training. They knew that when the chakras were open and unblocked, the body would resonate at a higher vibratory rate – a divine vibration.

Although the chakra system dates back at least to Medieval India, it was a popular consideration during the 1920s and 1930s in the U.S., one of many metaphysical doctrines espoused by the Spiritualist movement. The chakras were also noted in the work of Carl Jung, and Martha Graham – who had undergone Jungian analysis – based her dance technique on the activity of the chakras. Yet, this information is usually ignored historically.

The Japanese Butoh dancer, Maureen Fleming, speaks about this interior transformation in her own dancing. "A lot of the images in Butoh works at opening these chakras. When the chakra centers are open, there is a real experience of transformation in the body that is not anything about the experience, but is the experience. You feel physically different. You feel emotionally different and it's a kind of catharsis."[24]

This state of transcendence, whereby dancers receive divine energies in their own bodies, vis à vis the chakras, is a form of healing, re-balancing, aligning. The body can be a trusted form of spiritual intelligence, if we pay attention, although that idea has been misaligned for centuries. Using fire, music, herbs, symbols, and prayerful offerings to their goddess, ancient peoples evoked a natural opening of the chakras and thus created a healing ritual. Ritualistic practices have always had their roots in healing. In our technological age, many of the rituals of the past have been forgotten because our lives have become too hectic and filled. Isadora Duncan, Ruth St. Denis and Martha Graham used their creative works as did the shamans and *curanderos* who sanctify the process of healing incorporating a spiritual perspective. They offered their audiences an opportunity to be part of sacred healing space and to enter the magic of ceremony. "You have to have some relationship to the gods or to God. The theater to me is a very holy place – created by man's appetite and desire and his need for participation in all of the forces of life," wrote Martha Graham.[25]

A beautiful example of dance as a healing art occurred for one woman who saw her dance *Lamentation*, as Graham relates:

> *Lamentation*, my dance of 1930, is a solo piece in which I wear a long tube of material to indicate the tragedy that obsesses the body, the ability to stretch inside your own skin, to witness and test the perimeters and boundaries of grief, which is honorable and universal. I was backstage, changing out of my costume and removing my make-up, when there was a knock at my door. A woman entered my dressing room. She had obviously been crying a great

The Pieta *in Kloster Andechs by Roman Anton Boos.*

Yet once more I shall die as man, to soar
With the blessed angels; but even from angelhood
I must pass on. All except God perishes.
– Aldous Huxley, The Perennial Philosophy.

deal and she said to me, "You will never know what you have done for me tonight. Thank you." She left before I could get her name. Later, I learned that she had recently seen her nine-year-old son killed by a truck before her eyes. She was unable to cry. No matter what was done for her she was not able to cry until she watched *Lamentation*. What I learned that night is that there is always one person in the audience to whom you speak. One.[26]

Although I have never seen Graham in this work, I did have the opportunity to watch it and write about it when her company was touring the West Coast several years ago. It left me speechless, utterly filled with profound sadness for ruins in my own life. Graham created the piece after studying artist Käthe Kollwitz's drawings of the ravages of World War I, and in the choreography she focused on the universal themes of loss, and personal and collective pain. *Lamentation* is an enduring homage and a powerful ritualistic vehicle in which the audience members (even just one audience member) could grieve their own devastations.

Dorothy Bird, one of the original members of Martha Graham's company, wrote about the work:

Martha's masterpiece, *Lamentation*, encapsulated feelings of frustration helplessness and utter grief. But in *Lamentation* the grief has been stoically born, communicated through economic movements, performed with an often hidden, impassive mask of the face. The expressiveness of Martha's open throat and twisting feet was far more effective than any facial expression could ever have been. All other parts of her body were shrouded by a long, unfitted tube of grayish-blue wool jersey that she stretched and twisted violently from within.

Her veiled, suppressed feelings constantly passed through the fabric in this rhapsodic song of grief.[27]

Ritual by definition is "the manner of providing divine service." It provides us with the opportunity to align with our soul-force, to inhabit a world of emotions, of feelings, of meaning, a world that most of us rarely engage fully. Martha Graham, Isadora Duncan, and Ruth St. Denis gave their audiences the chance to dwell in a divine world and to offer divine service. Through their own female bodies, they offered themselves as potent and primary vehicles for psychological and spiritual transformation. Ruth St. Denis explained her own metamorphosis from artist to priestess when she wrote: "My approach to the performance was at least a half hour of meditation. My maid would dress me in the elaborate costume [for Radha], hang my jewels about me, put my wig on carefully, and set my crown. Then, when I was completely ready, I would put her out, shut the door, and for a brief thirty minutes realize my contact with the one Mind, and through an inner discipline, seek to dissolve the lingering, irritations, personal relationships, and the petty human atmosphere which inevitably accompanied me to my dressing room. By the time I had left to go on the stage I was truly the priestess in the temple."[28]

Women in Religious Dance

Women are more in sync with their energetic capabilities simply because they experience the internal workings of their bodies through menstrual cycling and the choice of childbirth. The female body has always been a vehicle for experiencing this alignment and has been "perceived as a doorway which allows access to spiritual and psychic dimensions not normally visible. Perhaps, that accounts for women's overwhelming presence in shamanistic rites and the fact that in Japan, shamanism is practiced almost exclusively by women."[29] Women shamans in China often invited "possession," wherein the spirits of the dead were offered refuge in their bodies in the midst of Sacred dances. They would "invite into themselves (spirits) by dancing in circles until they induced a state of trance. In order to properly

Ruth Harwood's visual depiction of Ruth St. Denis's poem, "Crusader." Courtesy of The Ruth Harwood Papers, Manuscripts Division, Marriott Library, University of Utah.

receive this spirit into her body, the shaman purified herself with perfumed water, clothed herself in ritual costume, and made an offering."[30]

Non-Christian priestesses were able (and are able) to transpose the experiences of the "inside" into form through the sacred dance. Their gestural language occurred through the rhythm of the dance and, coupled with singing and chants, became the first primal form of worship. The priestesses were able to "awaken people's inner lives of soul by communicating to them the tones, sounds, and rhythms of nature. As the power of these priestesses grew stronger, the people around them could not do otherwise than begin to move. They had to start making rhythmic, dance-like movements, thus giving rise to rhythmic dances."[31] Fertility dances, belly dances and dances of initiation all contain the dynamics of being spun, whirled, or shaken, and often the participants dropped from utter exhaustion.

The maenads were one of the many female cults who embodied the idea of receiving feminine spiritual energies through their bodies. Originating from the Greek, meaning "mad woman," this definition is reflective of the perceived nature of maenads as wild women who had lost contact with reality and were believed to be under the control of the god, Dionysus. In the account written by Euripedes, the "women were free with a bountiful world of nature magically at their command."[32] They danced so ecstatically (with their entire being), that they were considered "crazy" and out of control to those who observed them. These beings, half-mythological and half-human, danced for days at a time with an ecstatic passion that defied their bodies ability and stamina. Through the dance they were transformed into an ecstatic frenzy because it was believed that the goddess had actually entered into their bodies, controlling their minds and physicality. "From a religious standpoint, these dance rites were not viewed as a mere human diversion, but seen as a serious attempt to gain contact with the god[dess]. From a more psychological point of view, maenadism represented a relaxation of rational self-control and a chance to be free of the partriarchally imposed definitions of Self, womanhood and sanity."[33]

This "state" was known as *en-theos-iasmos*, or the state of having the god within one.[34] The word "enthusiasm" derives from this Greek word. Plutarch wrote that these "women left the city at night in the winter, wandered for days without much food, held ritual dances at various stopping points and this strain on the body and exhaustion, as well as the suggestive use of music, are what the maenads used to 'induce an altered state of consciousness.'"[35] This altered state of consciousness is, of course, pivotal to the sacred dance experience.

Isadora Duncan especially identified with the maenads, and they were apt companions for her, since she, like them, defied conventions and the status quo. When she was in Berlin on tour, she wrote an editorial to the newspaper editor of the *Berlin Morgen Post*, upset by the negative reviews she had received, and she took advantage of this editorial opportunity to vent her anger.

> While reading your esteemed paper, I was embarrassed to find that you had asked so many admirable masters of the dance to expend such profound thought on so insignificantly a subject as my humble self. And I suggest that instead of asking them, "Can Miss Duncan dance?" you should have called their attention to a far more celebrated dancer – one who has been dancing in Berlin for years, long before I appeared: a natural dancer whose style (which I try to follow) is also in direct opposition to today's school of ballet.
>
> The dancer to whom I refer is the statue of the dancing Maenad in the Berlin Museum. Now, will you kindly write again to the admiral masters and mistresses of the ballet and ask them, "Can the dancing Maenad dance?" For the dancer of whom I

speak has never tried to walk on the end of her toes, neither has she spent time practicing leaps in the air to see how many times she could clap her heels together before coming down again. She wears neither corset not tights, and her feet rest freely in her sandals. I believe a prize has been offered to the sculptor who could replace the statue's broken arms in their original position. I suggest that it might be more useful, for art today, to offer a prize to whoever could reproduce in life the heavenly poise of her body and the secret beauty of her movement.[36]

During the fourth century AD, a group of women existed who called themselves the Collyridians. (I wonder if the derivation of their name may have stemmed from the worship of the Hindu goddess Kali?) These women worshipped the Virgin Mary as a form of the Divine Feminine, using dance in their ceremonies. They also ate round cakes made of honey, called *colenruada* or *collyrides*, as part of a ritual that was popular before Christ. Although the existence of these feminine worshippers of the "Goddess Mary" is documented historically only a handful of later texts even mention them. The idea of women worshipping Woman was heretical, and the Collyridians were condemned in the same manner that other female goddess-worshippers have been vilified.

The Collyridians lived in Thrace, located between what we now call Greece and Turkey, the same location where the dancing maenads lived. However, these sects were not confined to this area, and similar groups of women who worshipped the goddess were widespread in lands west and north of the Black Sea, Scythia and Arabia, although there is no evidence that it was an organized movement of women en masse. Ancient texts refer to them with animosity and fear.

In 373 AD, Epiphanus, the bishop of Salamis in Cyprus, wrote *The Panarion* or *Medicine Chest*,[37] a strange name for a book on heresy, which targeted women in general, and worshippers of the goddess in particular. His work is even more curious because he purportedly used the word "Collyridian" only as a nickname, as he was hesitant to reveal the true name of the sect. It is odd that a man with the rank of bishop would be afraid of this band of women. Certainly he could have exercised his religious powers to destroy them.

These Collyridians included men in their group rituals, and Epiphanus vilified the members citing them as " silly, weak and contemptible." Nevertheless, the cult spread quickly as assemblies and associations began worshipping Mary as Queen of Heaven.

"They adorn a chair or a square throne, spread a linen cloth over it, and, at a certain time, place bread on it and offer it in the name of Mary, and all partake of the bread," Epiphanus wrote, and the ceremony lasted for many days.[38] It is most likely that Epiphanus used the word "Collyridians" because it derived from the Greek word, *Kollyris*, or loaf of bread. The offerings of cakes of meal and honey to the Virgin "as if she, [the Virgin Mary] had been a divinity"[39] transferred to her, in fact, the worship that was previously paid to Ceres.

It is not clear from historical texts whether the Collyridians were punished or killed for their dance rituals, since these women posed a grave threat to the religious powers at that time. Epiphanus, listed "80 heresies in his book; Heresy No.70 was aimed at these women, saying, that after so many generations, women should not be appointed priestess. About Mary he said, "[God] gave her no charge to minister baptism or bless disciples, nor did he bid her rule over earth."[40] Geoffrey Ashe, in *The Virgin: Mary's Cult and the Re-Emergence of the Goddess*, states the rule differently: "Let the Father, the Son and the Holy Spirit be worshipped, but let no one worship Mary."

Although the Collyridians and various goddess-centered religions persisted in dancing their sacred rituals throughout history, these women defied the church's condemnation, and ironically, they were "excellent public relations for the

Church, since their practice mirrored the sacred ceremonies to the goddess and it was as if they transferred their 'pagan' goddess to a 'Christian' one. Christianity has a long tradition of integrating pagan practices. In exchange for tolerating widespread devotion to the Virgin Mary, the Church received a greater following and probably more converts they ever thought they would have."[41] Spanish missionaries dishonored the tradition of the Native American Indians in converting them to Catholicism. As a result of such coercion, the natives attended church in public, although privately they worshipped their own deities.

Dances to the Virgin

Little is written about the life of the Virgin Mary in the traditional Bible. Aside from private revelations, most of the historical information that exists about her is found in the Apocryphal Gospel of Provangelium, or Book of James, which was written between 100 and 150 AD. This book offers many provocative insights and details that were missing in sources up to that time, and contains the first known description of a dance not only *to* the Virgin Mary, but in fact, danced *by* the Virgin Mary herself when she was three years old. According to the text, her mother Anna (or Anne) and father Joachim decide to visit the temple and make an offering to God, since Anna is childless. When she becomes pregnant (with the Virgin Mary), as promised by an angel, Anna decides that she will dedicate the child to God.[42] In order to maintain the child's purity, her mother created a protected environment to ensure that her feet never touch the ground. She is carried by servants and family members at all times and even Mary's bedroom is off-limits to males, and only pure women are allowed to enter.[43]

Mary's parents take her to the temple when she is three years old, and she dances near the altar to the delight of all present. The actual text reads: "The priests placed her on the third step of the altar, and the Lord God put Grace upon the child, and she danced for joy with her feet, and all the house of Israel loved her."[44]

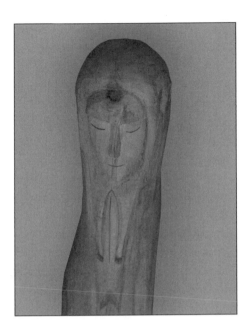

Image of the prayerful Virgin Mary carved out of wood.
Photograph taken in New Mexico by photographer Mark Roseman.

The young child continues to receive instruction from the priests until age thirteen, when they decide that she is "not fit" for further religious study because she is of menstruating age, and in Orthodox Judaism, young women are considered "unclean" when they have their periods. Therefore, she was not allowed to study the mystical texts of the Kabbalah. The text reads: "When she was twelve years old, a council of priests said: Behold Mary has become twelve years old in the temple of the Lord. What then shall we do with her lest she pollute the sanctuary of the Lord?"[45]

What makes this story even more remarkable is the fact that Iris Stewart, author of the wonderful book *Sacred Woman, Sacred Dance*, traveled to Crete and found artistic evidence that this was much more than a legend, but actually took place. "I found a rare depiction of this scene on the walls of an ancient Byzantine Church of the Virgin of Kera. Mary and her parents are accompanied by the Daughters of the Hebrews, whose regal costuming clearly indicated their status among the holy."[46]

Marian identification remained and has continued within various cultures all over the world that have transformed their goddess images into the Christian Goddess, the Virgin Mary. In 431 AD, she received the title of "Theotokos" or "The Bearer of God," although this title was controversial among those who wished to deny her a divine status – a status that is still ignored by many in the Christian religions.

> It is proper to call you blessed, ever-esteemed Theotokos, most pure, and Mother of God. You who are more worthy of honor than the cherubim and far more glorious than the seraphim. You who incorruptibly, gave birth to God, the Word, Theotokos, we fervently extol you. – St. John Chrysostom[47]

After the declaration of the Council of Ephesus proclaiming her the Mother of God, devotion to the Virgin Mary increased. The site of the religious council was also a sacred site to the goddess Diana, and a shrine was built to the Virgin Mary on the exact spot that Diana's temple had stood. The easy interchange between goddess images and the Virgin Mary was a keen acknowledgment of the mystical and divine powers of the sacred feminine, and that transference is validation of the inherent female authority as a dimension of the divine. "Each culture interpreted her in its own way. Stone Age people drew their goddess huge and nurturing. The sensuous Minoans put snakes into her hands. The hot-headed Celts set their goddesses on horseback and into deep rivers and told tales of them stalking the countryside. The classical Greeks made theirs intellectual; Rome's goddesses were versatile. Goddesses from distant lands wandered in and settled down, bringing new incense, exotic rites, and richly brown complexions."[48]

Ritual dance combined with chant and music is a form of sacred dance that still exists today. During the Middle Ages, when the round dance (also called a *chorea*) was at its peak of popularity, holidays honoring the Virgin's life were celebrated with dances to Mary. During church services of confirmation, young girls sang a hymn to her containing the following words: "Thou who made merry among the lilies, encircled by the ring-dance of the virgins."[49] The lily is a sacred symbol associated with the Virgin Mary and is used in Christian art as a symbol of purity, an attribute of the virgin saints. During the Renaissance, when the Virgin Mary was painted, and with the advent of the popularity of the Rosary, the rose became another sacred symbol. The Feast of the Roses of the Virgin Mary was a sacred ceremony in which participants sang a hymn to the Virgin Mary, while dancing in tandem with the song:

> Virgin, thou dost rise to everlasting triumph!
> Thou dost rightly share the heavenly ring-dance.
> Beautiful there, through the flower of virginity,
> Bearing the mantel of the sun of righteousness.[50]

During the twelfth century in Spain, after the recitation of the *Ave Maria* (the Rosary), a dance was performed by the congregants. A rare description of the ceremony, written in 1878, describes the dance.

> The Ave Maria has just been sung and the blessing and the sacrament administered, when *el baile de los seises*, the dance of the six began. The high altar glittered with candles and gold, the church was filled with organ music, the Archbishop has just raised the jeweled monstrance above the heads of the kneeling worshippers and there was complete silence. Then entered the choristers, dressed magnificently as

pages of the seventeenth century. Standing before the high altar, first they dropped to their knees, then they rose and sang a curious melodious song; then they put on their hats, divided into two groups and stepped backwards and forwards, making figures and singing, sometimes accompanying themselves with castanets. The dance resembled a minuet, lasted about a quarter of an hour and made a very remarkable spectacle. The deep reverence of the spectators emphasized the strangeness of the performance.[51]

It was not unusual for the blending of hymns and dance to go hand in hand, and this was certainly evident in many of the dances to the Virgin Mary especially during the early Middle Ages. Another hymn, recited to celebrate her birth, obviously incorporated singing and dance as it directed:

Now, clap in applause
Ye men and women
Tune up in harmony
Beautiful communal songs
and dance ring-dances
In holy Mary's honour.[52]

"Ye men and women" indicates that both genders participated in these dance rites, which echoed the dance celebrations of the ancients.

These ecstatic rites were so important to those who danced them because dancing provided people the physical form to achieve a transcendent state – that state also called "embodied knowledge," honoring the wisdom of the spiritual body. Across disciplines, according to dance ethnologist and performance studies scholar, Deirdre Sklar, "There is a growing acknowledgment that embodied knowledge is as important to verbal knowledge in cultural communication."[53] The purpose of these dances to the Virgin Mary

Mary and the Hebrew Maidens Dancing. From an early church manuscript drawing, Vatican Library. Courtesy of Iris J. Stewart.

resides in such "felt knowledge" experienced by the dancers. "When you are dancing it's the same as dancing with the Virgin. It's something like if I were talking to her, expressing my gratitude of what she has done. Everytime I am dancing it's like I am saying Thank you, and just talking to her and giving thanks."[54]

This at-one-ment with the Virgin Mary is one of the primary reasons that Isadora Duncan, Ruth St. Denis, and Martha Graham created their dances to her.

"Spirit of Isadora." Photograph of Lori Belilove, Artistic Director of the Isadora Duncan Dance Foundation. Photographer David Fullard. Courtesy of the Isadora Duncan Dance Foundation.

Chapter Two

Isadora Duncan

Gemini, Born May 26, 1877[1]

The ruler of Gemini is Mercury, the servant of Jupiter and messenger of the Gods, whose function is to reveal the mind of Deity to man. Her mission is expression, and her chief characteristics are versatility and adaptability. Her influences show in agility and body dexterity. Deity manifesting on the physical plane must express the Self in terms of that plane, limited and bounded by physical conditions; must build up a personality – an efficient body – by means of which expression is possible. Mercurians only strike the keynote of their being, JOY, when in the act of expressing some essential part of themselves. Theirs is a charming type, whose true function is to make life more interesting and more beautiful for themselves and others: to stimulate, refresh and revive their fellowman by force. Gemini is said to rule both the arms and the legs, and the breathing capacity should be carefully watched. It generally arouses in those under its influence certain wistful cravings connected with the spiritual element in human nature. Any modification of faculty or of character due to this mystic influence is certain to be interesting, and in the case of highly evolved Geminians might conceivably give very brilliant results, possibly connected with high achievement in the domain of music, literature, or art.[2]

Isadora clad in the little white tunic her mother had made, standing motionless, her hands crossed upon her breast, her eyes wide with some vision. She would stand, feeling its power pulsing through her and the she would begin to dance.[3] To see her dance was to experience a profound emotion. She dances; nothing else mattered. There was nothing else. She had no part to play, no steps to perform, no music. Yet the world fell down and worshipped. There has never been anything like it in the history of dancing, of the theatre, of art. They called her "the Holy Isadora."[4]

In the midst of emotional and financial upheaval, Mary Dora Duncan gave birth to her fourth child, a little girl she named Dora Angela Duncan. The infant's name would later change during baptism ceremonies into the now famous Isadora. Abandoned by her husband before Isadora was born, Mary Duncan (emotionally and financially bereft) was convinced that "This child will surely not be normal." When Isadora emerged "furiously agitating her arms and legs" during the birth, her mother cried, "You see I was quite right, the child is a maniac!" Although, Duncan was considered by some during her lifetime to be exactly that, her revolutionary ideas were quite simply years ahead of the times.

Duncan's life was extraordinary not only for the era she lived in, but for any era. Breaking the dictums of the day that demanded that women maintain a silent voice, often repressing their own psychological, sexual, and creative desires, Duncan's bohemian upbringing in San Francisco placed her synchronistically in an environment of cultural exploration that was a departure from the norm. Although her early life was filled with financial instability, she seemed to be a happy child, and enjoyed her mother's piano playing and poetry readings in the evenings. However, the lack of money and her mother's emotional distance, forced young Isadora to mature at an early age. Isadora hints at her mother's lack of formal parental regulations or participation in the following words: "There were no set times for rising or going to bed, nor any discipline in our lives. I think my mother quite forgot about us, lost in her music or declaiming poetry, oblivious to all around her."[5] However, this independence offered the child a freedom to explore her world, a freedom she took great delight in. "I had no toys or childish fun. I often ran away alone into the woods or to the beach by the sea, and there I danced."

She wrote in her autobiography that she believed that "whatever one is to do in one's life is clearly expressed as a baby." Declaring to her mother that she was "already a dancer and a revolutionist," when she was only six years old, Isadora told her mother that she would begin a dance school, and spent hours teaching the neighborhood children "how to wave their arms gracefully" even though many of the children could hardly walk.

Duncan taught dance in the neighborhood and helped the family earn a living by presenting concerts for the elite in San Francisco, something she would continue to do for financial gain throughout her life.

> The finest inheritance you can give to a child is to allow it to make its own way, completely on its own feet. Our teaching, led my sister and me into the richest houses in San Francisco. I did not envy these rich children; on the contrary, I pitied them. I was amazed at the smallness and stupidity of their lives, and, in comparison with these children of millionaires, I seemed to be a thousand times richer in everything that made life worthwhile.[6]

Her contempt for the public educational system would inform her later teaching philosophy because she believed that it "showed a brutal incomprehension of children."

Isadora Speaks

My mother came home one day and found that I had collected a half dozen babies of the neighborhood and had them sitting before me on the floor while I was teaching them to wave their arms. When she asked the explanation of this, I informed her that it was my school of the dance. She was amused and placing herself at the piano, she began to play for me. The school continued and became very popular. Later on, the little girls of the neighborhood came and their parents paid me a small sum to teach them. This was the beginning.
– ML, 14.

Often hungry and clad in wet clothing, Duncan was forced to sit still in classes while her teacher "an inhuman monster was there to torture us. And of these sufferings children will never speak." When she was ten years old, she put her hair up and told everyone that she was sixteen. Because she was so tall for her age, she was easily believed.

Isadora's childhood dance classes became so popular that at age ten she quit public school and concentrated on making money through her dance classes. One of the first dances she taught was based on Longfellow's poem, "I shot an arrow into the air." Duncan would recite the poem and instruct her students on the movement vocabulary. This improvised and emotional response to poetry and music permanently shaped her future philosophies.

When she attended ballet classes in San Francisco at the insistence of a friend, she hated the lessons. She wrote essays expressing her contempt for this dance form. Duncan fervently believed that "the art of the dance will be the study of the movements of Nature," and these natural forms of the body provided entry into the embodiment of truth and beauty. It was through this alignment that one could perceive the invisible Divine forces. Well-versed in the complete compendium of the arts – literature, sculpture, and music – Duncan understood that "the consciousness of its divinity are at the root of all arts created by man. A single artist has lost this divinity, an artist who above all would be first to desire it – the dancer."[7] The future of humankind, she believed, "which dreams of becoming God," was through the natural intelligence of the body.

Reading Was Her Passion

Duncan adored books and this passion would accompany her throughout her life. She spent countless hours in the public library and read the complete works of Dickens, Thackeray, Shakespeare, and "thousands of novels besides, good and bad, inspired books and trash – I devoured everything."[8] Although, she wasn't academically schooled by

Isadora Speaks

When the teacher asked me to stand on my toes I asked him why, and when he replied "Because it is beautiful," I said that it was ugly and against nature and after the third lesson I left his class, never to return. This stiff and commonplace gymnastics which he called dancing only disturbed my dream. I dreamed of a different dance. I did not know just what it would be, but I was feeling out towards an invisible world into which I divined I might enter if I found the key. My art was already in me when I was a little girl. – ML, 23.

traditional means, she was also an avid reader of William Blake, Charles Darwin, Plato, and Goethe, and her inordinate verbal as well as physical skills are notable. When she was in Paris, she described her love of the written word: "In addition to the two greatest sources of joy, the Louvre and the National Library, I now discovered a third: the charming library of the Opera. The librarian took an affectionate interest in my researches and placed at my disposal every work ever written on dancing, and also all the books on Greek music and Theatre art. I applied myself to the task of reading everything that had ever been written on the Art of Dancing, from the earliest Egyptians to the present day, and I made special notes of all I read in a copy-book."[9]

She Touched the World

Duncan's influence on the artists of her day were abundant. Erté, the famous artist, remembered her contributions. "With her sound musical intuition and taste she projected a visual interpretation of the spirit of the music to which she danced. She deserved all the adulation she received. During her lifetime, as well as after her death, she was a source of inspiration not only for dancers but for many other artists."[10]

The French sculptor Rodin believed that Isadora was "the greatest woman I have ever known, and her art has influenced my work more than any other inspiration that has come to me." The great dancer Vaslov Nijinsky credited her as "the great inspiration," and during one magic afternoon in a luncheon that they both attended, "After the table had been cleared away someone played the piano. And Isadora and Nijinsky danced together – Isadora creating the dance as the music flowed from the piano, and Nijinsky dancing with her as though she has rehearsed each entirely new measure for weeks. It was an amazing performance – Isadora's extraordinary power of instantaneous creation and Nijinsky's sensitive response to her mood and to the music."[11]

She inspired a vast number of prominent artists from a multitude of art forms including painters, sculptors, writers, and photographers, which speaks to her extraordinary range of artistic powers. Robert Henri, the father of the Ash-Can School of art, and a noted writer in his own right, wrote poetically about her influence. "When a great artist as Isadora Duncan, affects us, when we realize her, we are great as well as she."[12] Often called the "Barefoot Dancer," a term she loathed, Duncan not only revolutionized the modern dance form, established schools for dance embedded with her own accompanying spiritual and feminist philosophies, but was unafraid to explore and challenge the current art forms, forms that were in dire need of reshaping. Western theatrical dance during her era was replete with tightrope walkers, contortionists and music hall presentations that were little more than popular entertainment.

If Duncan had lived a natural life cycle, instead of dying at age fifty in an automobile accident, no doubt her mature voice would have extended her radical philosophies, continuing to be a major figure in the panoply of the artistic revolution in theatre, politics, and the arts that was taking place during the Jazz Age. Everything was topsy-turvy and ripe for change; the flappers flapped, musicians jazzed, and everything and anything that had been was simply not the order of the day anymore. The antiquated rules of the Victorian era in which she lived were eagerly tossed aside, while a new breed of artists and visionaries emerged to blaze their own paths of freedom with wild abandon. Women finally had the vote, birth control was available and it was fitting that one of the most popular songs of that time was "I Want to Be Bad." And Duncan often was – drinking and eating to excess, hiding from her hotel bills, donning flimsy and what was considered scandalous clothing *off* the stage, and offering a vocal voice on women's rights before the topic was part of the culture. She even performed onstage while visibly pregnant – and without a husband.

Isadora Speaks

When I spoke to an audience in Moscow, I implored them not to view children as little actresses against a backdrop of theatrical scenery. I wanted them to see them against a backdrop of nature, where they can dance freely on the meadow and among the trees.
–IS, 119.

Duncan did more than espouse spirited philosophies of freedom for women in their life's choices and dress, she lived her ideals. Her life was her truth. She demanded absolute respect for the female form, believed in sexual freedoms and was unashamed of being pregnant with her two children by two different men; the great English theatre innovator, Gordon Craig (father of her daughter Deirdre), and Paris Singer (father of her son Patrick), the dashing and incredibly wealthy heir to the American Singer Sewing Machine business, who would become her patron of the arts. Firmly rooted in her own power as a woman and artist, she didn't need permission to create her unorthodox life; she simply lived it because she couldn't imagine living any other way.

Although her romantic conquests would ebb and flow, no doubt being labeled as "the female Casanova of America"[13] by Spanish novelist and political activist Vicente Blasco Ibanez would have delighted her. Although she enjoyed the pleasures of the flesh, that did not negate her spiritual credo for the dance. Rather, these pleasures were an extension of her belief of the freedom and spontaneity of movement – of the human body. It makes perfect sense that she would carry this liberation into all aspects of her private life. Some of her critics mention her sexual conquests derogatorily, instead of understanding that *this* was a woman fully versed in all aspects of living – in body, in mind, and in spirit. She understood that as an artist she would foster contempt by the very nature of how she lived. "Every artist worth anything has always been vilified. It is the price the world demands for the beauty we invoke."[14]

Her Dance Was Her Religion

Although Isadora Duncan was not religious in the orthodox sense of the word, she believed that dance was her religion. The philosophy that dance would be a prayer, a holy state, was new to her audiences as well as to the producers of that time. Even during the earliest years of her professional dancing, Duncan declared her art a religion,

Isadora Speaks

And we must have Philosophy – Without that we would die of pain like dumb brutes. Some people draw it from one source & some from another. Some people pray one way & and some another – sometimes I dance mine & sometimes I think them. –YI, 97.

and she wanted to share those sacred moments with her audiences so that they would be able to spontaneously experience a higher state of consciousness. A self-taught artist, Isadora attributed her education to the Muse Terpischore, who guided her in her dancing.

Wassily Kandinksy, the German painter and writer, published widely on the subject of the link between spirituality and the arts. His book, *On the Spiritual in Art and Painting in Particular,* is perhaps his best known, although it is not clear if Duncan read it. However, what is clear is that Kandinsky was well aware of her.

> We are faced with the necessity of creating a new dance form, the dance of the future. The same law of exploiting uncompromisingly the inner sense of movement as the principal element of dance will produce its effect and lead us towards our goal. Conventional "beauty" of movement must be thrown overboard. Both arts must learn from music that every harmony and every discord which springs from the inner spirit is beautiful, but that it is essential that they should derive from the inner spirit and from that alone. We will soon be able to sense the inner value of every movement, and inner beauty will replace outer beauty…that now suddenly streams forth at once an undreamed of power and living strength.[15] [The dance] must be replaced by another capable of bringing forth subtler spiritual vibrations. Thus originated the link forged by Isadora Duncan between Greek dance and the dance of the future. In this she is working on parallel lines to the painters who are looking for inspiration among the primitives.[16]

Kandinsky and Duncan were kindred spirits recognizing nature as the impetus for their inspiration in their work. Both artists were driven by an internal force that commanded them to create. For them it was not simply an exercise in the creative process, it was a necessity for their psychological survival. A pantheist, Isadora drew her inspiration largely from nature, which was also one of her religious precepts. "True dance comes from the patterns of nature in which Isadora saw a distilled wave movement running through all natural phenomena, including the human body. This wave movement was created by an alternating current of gravity in its attraction and resistance to matter which the dancer concentrated in the place or site of the body, thus explaining the need to release the body from all artificially imposed restrictions. This perception of the dancer as part of nature, capable of channeling nature into creative human expression, philosophically contradicted the idea of humans as beings set apart from nature and endowed with a God-given right to dominate nature. Duncan's dancer accepts her place in nature and opens herself up to its forces, to translate the knowledge of nature passing through her, taking up the philosophical thread of the matriarchal world which also processed the forces of nature in the interest of the body.[17]

Kandinsky and Duncan shared the revelation that the spectator (either in dance or painting) was an *active recipient* in the sense that the recipient or audience member should listen to his or her inner prompting instead of searching for the proper "meaning" of the painting. These inner promptings are an integral component of the spiritual quest, an activity that mystics often refer to as *"trusting the God within."* This guiding intuitive voice has always been the foundation for sacred art, *if*, and, *when* artists allow themselves to surrender to their personal spiritual voices.

The spectator is all too accustomed to seek a "meaning," i.e., an external connection between the parts of the painting. Once again, in life in general and therefore also in art, this same materialistic period produced the spectator who is unable simply to relate to the picture (especially true of connoisseurs),

Isadora Speaks

Dancing, through a long era lacked all sense of elemental natural movement. It tried to afford the sense of gravity overcome – a denial of nature. Its movements were not living, flowing, undulating, giving rise inevitably to other movements. All freedom and spontaneity were lost in a maze of intricate artifice. Then, when I opened the door to nature, revealing a different kind of dance, some people explained it all by saying, "See it is natural dancing." But with its freedoms, its accordance with natural movement, there was always a design too – even in nature you find sure, even rigid design. "Natural" dancing should mean only that the dance never goes against nature, not that anything is left to chance. – TAOD, 79.

and who looks for everything possible in the painting; what he does not attempt is to experience for himself the inner life of the picture, to let the picture affect him directly. His spiritual eye is unable to seek out what it is that lives by these means.[18]

I have always deplored the fact that I was forced to dance in a theatre where people paid for their seats; a theatre with its stupid box-like stage and where the spectator's attitude is that of people who sit still and look but do not participate. Of course, in moments of great enthusiasm when the audience arises and applauds, they manifest a degree of dance participation. But I have dreamed of a more complete dance expression on the part of the audience, at a theatre in the form of an amphitheater, where there would be no reason why, at certain times, the public should not arise and by different gestures of dance, participate in my invocation.
– TAOD, 123.

Duncan felt strongly that her audiences should experience the "inner life of the dance." Not only were her ideas visionary, but by declaring her art a religion and appointing herself as high priestess of that art, she offered her dances to her audience as prayers.

The dancer of the future will be one whose body and soul have grown so harmoniously together that the natural language of that soul will have become the movement of the body. She will realize the mission of woman's body and the holiness of its parts. The highest intelligence in the freest body.[19]

Isadora provided her audiences an opportunity to be part of the spiritual atmosphere that she created on the stage and she wanted them to "feel and act upon the great forces transpiring in her."[20] It is telling that, at her first audition in San Francisco, when she appeared before theatre managers, they told her that "she was beautiful but that her art had nothing to do with theatre and that she should dance in a church."[21] Obviously, from her earliest days, Duncan's crystal-clear and authentic philosophies of dance were already apparent. Movement, for her, was the perfect vehicle to align mind, body and spirit, an alignment that echoed dance's earliest intention as a sacred act.

The Mystic at Work

Duncan's work, however, was not always joyful. Like many other artists, past and present, she struggled with the same angst of creating that often accompanies that process. Among the enormous cache of letters to her lover Gordon

Craig, she wrote: "I practice a little each day. The beginning is like breaking stones. One loves to work when once begun, but is it so difficult to reach the right state to begin – sometimes I wish I might dissolve into a mist rather than begin again – The feminine spirit has a special aversion to entering into that land of abstract idea where work is – Indeed only a few in History have succeeded in doing it alone and then only through suffering, and I object to suffer. To wrench oneself from Time and place and self and enter where time and space and self do not exist – that is a great pain – but then also a great reward. Is anything comparable to the feeling of having come in contact with that eternal idea of Beauty – a wrench, an awful suffering, a feeling of battering for ages against an impassable barrier, and then suddenly and sharply a glow, a light, a connection with the idea like entering into a God. [22] Trying to reconcile Spirit to Matter."[23]

What is immediately apparent in Duncan's text is how similar her spiritual struggle and attainment of an ecstatic state is to many of the mystic's experiences. Many artists experience being "lost in the artistic process," whereby all time and space cease. That ecstatic state is the same for mystics longing for union with the Divine. Both mystics and artists suffer: the longing for the idea – the poem – the dance – the painting; and after that struggle ends, the surrender begins in which the artist can give herself to the ecstatic state, to be lost in her art. Further, it wasn't enough for Duncan to experience these states; she was able to use her wisdom (derived from the process of making her dances) as the mystic would pen his thoughts about an exalted state.

Duncan's ecstatic states provided her with the same outcome of the mystical experience: *knowledge*. "Although so similar to states of feeling, mystical states seem to those who experience them to be also states of knowledge. They are states of insight into depths of truth unplumbed by the discursive intellect."[24] That knowledge, in Isadora's case, took form. She recognized that it was her role to be the messenger for the divine dance.

Isadora Speaks

There are those [dancers] who convert the body into a luminous fluidity, surrendering it to the inspiration of the soul, who understands that the body by the force of the soul, can be converted to a luminous liquid. When, in its divine power, it completely possesses the body, it converts that into a luminous moving cloud, and thus can manifest itself in the whole of its divinity…Imagine then a dancer who, after long study, prayer and inspiration, has attained such a degree of understanding that his body is simply the luminous manifestation of his soul; whose body dances in accordance with a music heard inwardly, in an expression of something out of another, a profounder world. This is the truly creative dancer. – TAOD, 51-52.

Isadora Speaks

There are two classes of dancing; sacred and the profane. By profane, I do not mean sinful, but simply that dancing which expresses the physical being and the joy of the senses, whereas sacred dancing expresses the aspirations of the spirit to transform itself into a higher sphere than the terrestrial. Very little is known of the magic which resides in movement, and the potency of certain gestures. In childhood, we feel the religious sense of movement poignantly, for the mind is not yet entirely clouded with dogmas and creeds. Children give themselves up entirely to the celebration and worship of the unknown, God, "Whatever gods may be." – TAOD, 124.

She succeeded in not only shedding the balletic style that required a movement lexicon that was unnatural to the human form, but spread her gospel of the dance in every aspect of her life through performances, lectures, published articles, books and training at her unique dance schools. Clearly, Duncan's contributions as a spiritual philosopher were quite similar to those of the other philosophers of her time, including Rudolf Steiner, yet, she was not then, nor even now, considered a "serious thinker."

Although Duncan translated the wisdom of the spirit into the wisdom of the body, it is shameful that her legacy of spiritual contributions is not considered with the same respect that mystics of the ages have been accorded. Her contributions to the mystical realm were the very foundations for the expansion and elevation of the art of dance. Her holistic dance training, a training that incorporated mind, body, and spirit, gave her students an opportunity to *feel* internally, the majesty and beauty of movement.

If only I had envisioned the dance as my Solo, my way would have been quite simple. Already famous, sought after in every country, I had only to pursue a triumphal career. But, alas! (I was possessed by the idea of a school – I was possessed by the dream of a Promethean creation that, at my call, might spring from the Earth, descend from the Heavens, such dancing figures as the world had never seen. Ah, proud, enticing dream that has led my life from one catastrophe to another! Why did you possess me?) Leading, like the light of Tantalus, only to darkness and despair. But no! Still flickering in that light in the darkness must eventually lead me to the Glorious Vision, at last realized. I still believe, I still follow you – to find those superhuman creatures that in Harmonious Love will dance the Great Vision of Beauty the world awaits.[25]

Metaphysical Connections

The late 1800s and the early 1900s witnessed an enormous revival of interest in metaphysics, and groups studying mysticism, alchemy, Rosicrucian philosophies and other spiritual/metaphysical teachings, including the works of Rudolf Steiner, Wassily Kandinsky,[26] Gurdijieff, and Madame Blavantsky, the founder of the popular Theosophy movement sprung up throughout the U.S. and Europe. Kandinsky's groundbreaking essay "Concerning the Spiritual in Art" was published in English in 1912 and Duncan, a voracious reader, probably read it.

Joséphin Péladan, art critic, writer, and a Catholic occultist, was one of the leaders of the Rosicrucian order, an order of mysticism that continues to enjoy a following today. During the late 1800s, he held salons in which he espoused the trinity of the artist's role – the fusion of art, religion, and occultism. He defined the artist in a way that appropriately described Duncan's art and vision:

> Artist, thou art priest[ess]: Art is the great mystery; and if your attempt turns out to be a masterwork, a divine ray descends upon the altar. Artist thou art king; art is the real kingdom. Drawing of the spirit, outline of the soul, form an understanding, you embody our dreams. Artist thou art magician: art is the great miracle and proves our immortality.[27]

The Theosophical Society was active all over the world. Their members held to the doctrine that "inner knowledge was the vehicle for understanding the Spirit."[28] Theosophy contends to be a synthesis of all religions, to have arrived at their inner, esoteric meaning, and implicitly, to be the highest of all religions. "Its principle doctrines are a pantheistic evolution and reincarnation, while the only morality it demands is an adhesion to the brotherhood of man."[29] In reading Duncan's writings, it is abundantly clear that she was acutely influenced by an inspired personal knowledge of the Divine.

Profoundly influenced by the metaphysical and spiritual revolution that was taking place around her all over the world, when she was in Greece, Duncan read the *Mysteries of Eleusis*: "Those mysteries of which no tongue can speak. Only blessed is he whose eyes have seen them: his lot after death is not as the lot of other men!"[30] She visited Monte Verita, an innovative (yet considered "radical"), community in Switzerland dedicated to "vegetarianism, socialism and mysticism." No doubt upon her visit she was privy to lectures by Hugo Ball and Hans Arp, key figures in the Dada movement. Ball believed that the mystical language of the world was to be found in children and in "hypnotic spells of mystical texts." He also aligned mysticism with radical politics, ideas that Duncan certainly embraced. Her lover at the time, Gordon Craig (son of famous actress Ellen Terry), was a member of The Hermetic Order of the Golden Dawn, a metaphysical group, and he frequently attended meetings with his sister and mother.[31] Of course, Craig and Duncan would discuss the ideas of this secret mystical/occultist organization devoted to the study of esoteric spiritual traditions.

Opening the Gates for Woman

Duncan possessed a steadfast belief in her own rare talents, and fashioned her life and art as she saw fit with little need or care for societal approval. She fervently supported freedom for women in all respects – mind, body and soul – a revolutionary idea at the time. Attempting to liberate women from the constriction of corsets, petticoats, long sleeves, high collars, and heavy skirts commonly worn by the women of her day, she chose comfortable tunics and sandals instead. She would often write and lecture about the sanctity of the human form, particularly the female form insisting that nature was the highest teacher.

A liberating force both in dance and in feminism, Isadora succeeded in breaking down the moral barriers regarding how a woman should live. She broke the rules her

Vintage photography of Isadora Duncan in classic pose taken by Raymond Duncan in the Theatre of Dionysus, Greece, 1903. Courtesy of the Isadora Duncan Dance Foundation.

entire life, and paid a high price for that rule breaking. Living a life true to her own doctrines, Duncan believed in the freedom of a woman's body in dance, in costume, and in sexual choices. Met with criticism both privately and publicly for her "nakedness" on stage, she initiated scandal wherever she went for her non-traditional outlook and philosophies.

Duncan spoke openly about women's rights, especially as those rights related to a woman's freedom of choice regarding her own body. These ideas were beginning to gather a base in America during the Suffrage movement, but Isadora did not wait for legal permission. Her famous quip about marriage, "Any intelligent woman who reads the marriage contract, and then goes into it, deserves all of the consequences," is still quoted today.[32] Her writings about women and their bodies are eerily prophetic, and still speak to women even though Isadora penned them almost eighty years ago.

> Oh Woman, come before us, before our eyes longing for beauty, and tired of the ugliness of civilization, come in simple tunics, letting us see the line and harmony of the body beneath, and dance for us. Dance us the sweetness of life. Dance for us the holiness of the woman's body. Give us again the sweetness and the beauty of the true dance, give us again the joy of seeing the simple unconscious pure body of a woman. Like a great call it has come, and women must hear it and answer it.[33]

She knew that it was "through the eyes of beauty that one most readily finds a way to the soul, but here is another way for women – perhaps an easier way – and that is through the knowledge of their own bodies."[34] Duncan wanted women to experience their bodies from an interior realm, a realm of knowing, of trust, so that they could be in touch with their own natural rhythms. For women today, who find themselves tyrannized by self-hatred for their bodies, with images

Isadora Speaks

Woman is not a thing apart and separate from all other life, organic or inorganic. She is just a link in the chain, and her movement must be one with the great movement which runs through the universe. I believe she shall be sculpture not in clay or marble but in her own body. If my art is symbolic for any one thing, it is symbolic of the freedom of woman and her emancipation from the hide-bound conventions that are the warp and woof of Puritanism. I would rather dance completely nude than strut in half-clothed suggestiveness as many women do today. To expose one's body is art; concealment is vulgar. When I dance, my object is to inspire reverence, not to suggest anything vulgar. I do not appeal to the lower instincts of mankind. – IS, 44, 48.

Isadora Duncan Study by Abraham Walkowitz. Pastel on olive green paper. n.d. (ca. 1917) Courtesy of University Gallery, University of Delaware, gift of Virginia Zabriskie.

of anorexic models portraying unreal images of beauty, Duncan is still an apt role model.

In Duncan's era, her insistence in being clothed in free-flowing tunics and sandals was scandalous. In shunning the corsets women wore at the beginning of the twentieth century, she believed that once you unlocked the suffocating garments of the time, you could unlock the creative energies of women. Frequently vilified when she danced as a participant in "terrible orgies," Duncan was not afraid to hold her ground. Appearing in Germany in a performance of the opera *Tannhaüser*, she wore a transparent tunic that showed all of her body. After the performance, one of her friends begged her to wear a scarf beneath her costume but Duncan refused. "I was adamant. I would dress and dance exactly my way, or not at all."[35]

Color, Light, and the Dance

The inter-relationships among gestures, images, colors, sacred geometry, and scents as vehicles for spiritual understanding have been studied, written about, and explored by many spiritual sects. A mind that was naturally receptive to such occult or spiritual experiences would grasp these concepts easily, and Duncan possessed such a mind. She was not only a dancer, but practiced yoga, a discipline that can often heighten the metaphysical/mystical state.[36]

Gordon Craig, Isadora's partner and a theatrical scenic artist, was interested in using a symbolic approach to stage design, which incorporated a synesthetic model, blending the various elements of all of the arts in order to produce an evocative and trance-like effect. He staged a production called "Theatre of Mood and Movement,"[37] devising "more abstract designs made of panels of gauze lit by electric lights. The color of the lighting would change in conjunction with the mood of the action, the rhythms of the actors' movements, and the tempo of the all-enveloping musical score. The end result was an evocative, moody production that created its effects as much through the synesthetic manipulation of expressive sound, color, and movement as through the narrative."[38]

Duncan wanted to develop her own ideas for a synesthetic model using color harmony and light in collaboration with the brilliant Russian composer Scriabine. She wrote: "He was not only a great composer, but had the vision of complete musical expression in form, color and movement.

Isadora Speaks

You see, I have been writing about dance waves, sound waves, light waves – all the same. How many thousands of miles an hour do light and sound waves travel? Distance doesn't matter because the supply is never ceasing. It's all a matter of magnetic forces – same things that keep the earth circling around the sun in constant rhythmical waves of attraction and repulsion making the Complete Harmony. I do not doubt that someday someone will discover an instrument which will do for sight what radio does for hearing, and we will discover that we are surrounded, not only by sounds, but also and invisibly, to our eye, by the presence of all that is no longer. – LUA 76, 181.

When I had the joy of meeting him in Moscow in 1912 and telling him my ideas for a school and a temple, he told me that the ideal of his life was to build such a temple in India, where at the same time, with full orchestral harmonies, the audience would be bathed in colors. Alas, the war and his early death cut this short. I do not know whether Scriabine has ever written anything definite about his plans for uniting color, light and movement in an apotheosis of beauty, but I am convinced that one day his genius will find its expression through some medium. [39]

Duncan was significantly influenced by the writings of the philosopher and poet Goethe, who created a color system that penetrated the mystical implications of individual colors. In his book, *Theory of Colour,* he wrote about the effects upon the soul of various color forms. Duncan wrote to Craig that, after she was bored into a state of stillness by reading Nietzche, "My brain will go pop. Only Goethe's *Conversations with Eckermann* eased me up considerably. These would please you – speaks a good deal over his color theory."[40]

The idea of visionaries as theologians of color is not a new idea. "It is impossible even to imitate the history of the theology of color. It occupies a much larger place in the history of Western theology than is usually expressed, it extends from the earliest inceptions of Christian theology among the apostolic fathers right into the beginnings of modern [science]."[41] Consider that Christ is often referred to in spiritual schools as "White-Light," or "Christ-Light," an appropriate correlation as white signifies ultimate purity. Even the word "soul" is derived from Sol or Sun: the Light-Center. The Bhagavad Gita speaks of the Imperishable Light – "Behold the Form of me various in kind, various in Colours" – and according to the Hindu sages, God is "The Shining One."

Several references to white as a symbol of the holiness of life are also found in the Bible. White is the color (or absence of color) that is worn by the Virgin Mary in paintings of the

"Immaculate Conception" and "Presentation in the Temple." The Roman vestal virgins wore white to signify innocence and purity, and this custom has evolved into the wearing of white for bridal dress.

From early childhood, Duncan possessed an acute awareness of nature, and this awareness of the colors in nature influenced her both consciously and unconsciously, particularly when making choices for the colors of her costumes and the lighting used on her stage. This idea for the unification of color with spirit, was part of Duncan's genius, for she understood that through "color harmonies" she would be able to reveal the spirit. "And finally one can well imagine that colour has a mystical significance...the many colours are suggestive of primeval conditions which belong equally to man's perceptions as to Nature, so there can be no doubt that they are able to serve us as a language."[42]

Echoing Duncan's philosophies, Frederich Christoph Oetinger, the founder of Christian theosophy, wrote about these correlations. "Color, chroa, chrus, chroma yet in Holy revelation everything is full of colors, and such things are of the essence...we see images of the eternal power of God, which is always at work, in all the plants, flowers, trees and vegetations."[43]

The color harmonies Isadora Duncan was probably referring to in her study are the "cosmic rays," or currents of spiritual forces that emanate from the "Divine White Light." These light rays are thought to be as essential to the existence of the etheric body as air is to the physical body. "Colour is a Divine Power, therefore a vital force. It works through us and in us, in every cell, nerve, gland and muscle; it shines in our auras and radiates upon us from the atmosphere. Colour is an active power, exerting a tremendous influence on the mental consciousness, the soul and the spirit. The value of a force such as Colour is that in essence it is spiritual."[44]

Light and Loie Fuller

Although Duncan's prominence overshadowed her contemporary, dancer/illusionist Loie Fuller, the two met in Berlin where Fuller was appearing. A pioneer, Fuller explored color and light, and experimented with this new technology to create expansive and compelling light shows. She danced on-stage with gigantic silk veils, experimenting with a machine that created the illusion of light appearing on the body in fluid patterns. Fuller's stage crew was enormous and she often had more than sixty electricians changing various colored gelatins underneath the stage, prompted by her musical dance responses. If you consider that this experimentation and presentation was years before the notion of "performance art," this was an amazing achievement. She, like Duncan was an imaginative trailblazer of what dance could "look like" on the stage. When Duncan met Fuller personally in Berlin, she was infatuated. "I went every night to see Loie Fuller and I was more and more enthusiastic about her marvelous ephemeral art," Duncan wrote. "That wonderful creature – she became fluid; she became light; she became every color and flame, and finally she resolved into miraculous spirals of flames wafted toward the Infinite."[45]

Duncan and the Goddess

During Duncan's era, the spiritualist movement was quite popular, as was the study of esoteric philosophies and religion. She had a particular affinity for the Egyptian goddess Isis, as do many women today. Also deemed the Queen of Heaven, many scholars believe [as I do] that the Virgin Mary, Isis, and other feminine deities are the same manifestation of the sacred and divine Feminine. Isis was considered the goddess of the wisdom nature, or creative principle, and a potent symbol of feminist thought.

Although Isis was regarded as the universal Mother, she was the patroness of women in particular. As the

Giver of Life, who presided over both birth and death, she was the protectoress of women in child-birth and the comforter of the bereaved. Isis' very human emotions and the qualities of love, compassion, tenderness and perseverance which she exemplified endeared her especially to the hearts of women. In Isis, women found a source of support and inspiration for their own lives. Isis proclaimed herself in ancient hymns as the Goddess of women and endowed women with power equal to that of men. She has been called one of the first exponents of women's liberation.[46]

Duncan's alignment with the goddess Isis is important, and this identification was also shared by Ruth St. Denis. According to the mystic Hilda Charlton, Isis was the symbol of the Divine Mother or bringer-forth of the perfect indwelling Self within us. In Charlton's prayer to Isis, she wrote: "I am She who is the Goddess of women. I have instructed mankind in the mysteries. I, Isis, am all that has been, that is or shall be; no mortal man hath ever Me unveiled."[47] Charlton also writes about the Virgin Mary, and the parallels between the two deities are apparent. "She [Mary] stands as an inspirational symbol of womanhood deified while yet in a human form. This related Her to the World-Mother concept of the divine creative principle."[48] During a train trip in 1905 with Gordon Craig, she played a game in which she would "talk" by writing her thoughts down on paper and then hand the sketch pad to him so he could "answer" her.[49] "I am called Isadora," she wrote. "That means child of Isis – or *Gift* of Isis. Isis is the Goddess of Birth – Isis will always protect me because I have her name. This is the 15 of January 1905. *Isis Protect Me.*"[50]

This short note confirms not only Duncan's knowledge of the goddess, but in her last words "*Isis Protect Me,*" penned a year before the birth of her first child, Deirdre, Duncan may have been utilizing her words as powerful affirmations associated with the veneration of the goddess. Historically, when Isis declared, "Come to Me, for My Speech hath in it the power to protect and it possesseth life,"[51] Duncan may have intuitively sought protection for her soon-to-be born child.

Ave Maria

Clearly, Duncan was drawn to the Virgin Mary, enough to make a dance called *Ave Maria* in her honor. The dance was performed to the accompaniment of Shubert's *Ave Maria*. She also chose *Ave Maria* as the hymn to be sung during her funeral procession.[52] Duncan's *Ave Maria* was not the only dance that she created using images from the celestial or goddess realm. She also choreographed *Cherubim* and *Mother*.

The concept of the Virgin Mary as progenitor of the creative principle may explain Duncan's calling to her dance, *Ave Maria*, and I agree with Mary Daly that "the image of Mary as Virgin…has an unintended aspect of pointing toward independence for women…The woman who is defined as virgin is not defined exclusively by her relationships with men…The message of *independence* in the Virgin symbol can itself be understood apart from the matter of sexual relationships with men.[53] The idea of the Virgin or goddess as independent woman would certainly have resonated with Duncan's philosophies.

However, it most certainly was her identification with the Sorrowful Mother – the Mary who lost her son – that struck a painful chord when Duncan's two children, Deirdre and Patrick were killed in a bizarre car accident. *Ave Maria*, one of her most enduring works, was created a year after the tragedy. In an undated letter to her students, she wrote of the consolation that dance gave her and instructed them to "dance only that music which goes from the soul in mounting circles."[54]

Plunge your soul in divine unconscious *Giving* deep within it, until it gives to your soul its *Secret.* That is how I have always tried to express music. My soul should become one with it, and the dance born from that embrace. Music has been in all my life the great Inspiration and will be perhaps the Consolation, for I have gone through such terrible years. No one has understood since I lost Deirdre and Patrick how pain has caused me at times to live in almost a delirium. When you think of those years, think of the *Funeral March* of Schubert, the *Ave Maria*, the *Redemption,* and forget the times when my poor distracted soul trying to escape the suffering may well have given you the appearance of madness. I have reached such high peaks flooded with light, but my soul has not strength to live there…Someday if you understand sorrow you will understand too all I have lived through, and then you will only think of the light towards which I have pointed and you will know the real Isadora is there. In the meantime work and create Beauty and Harmony. The poor world is in need of it.[55]

In 1907, eight years before the children's deaths Duncan appeared in a play as the Virgin Mary. Craig, her then-lover, bought her a statue of the Madonna while she was in preparation for this role as Madonna in a mystery play in Paris. She wrote to him: "I have the Madonna you brought me and she is lovely."[56] The play was called "Madonna of Leonardo de Vinci," and was performed a few weeks before Easter. In the finale of the program, "She, as the Madonna, slowly ascended a great staircase of Golgotha at the foot of the Cross, formed by spotlights against a black background. She was transformed."[57]

The parallels between Duncan and the Virgin Mary are notable. Each of these women knew in advance that her child (or children) would die, each of them was an

Isadora Duncan in Ave Maria.
Photographer Arnold Genthe. Courtesy of the Jerome Robbins Dance Division, The New York Public Library for the Performing Arts, Special Collections, Astor, Lenox and Tilden Foundation.

inspirational figure in the world, and each maintains a legendary status. Of course, Isadora Duncan and the Virgin Mary were also the center of philosophical thought: Duncan in the philosophy of the dance, and the Virgin Mary in the center of theological thought. Finally, each woman was both a visionary and a teacher.

Hail Mary

The historical influences in Isadora Duncan's masterpiece, *Ave Maria*, shed light on why she chose to create this work. Schubert's *Ave Maria* is remarkable, not only because it is a magnificent piece of music, but also because of its inherent healing powers. These were no doubt understood by Duncan, who was a connoisseur of great music. "The *Ave Maria* of Schubert is a transcription of the Blessed Virgin's musical soul-pattern. It vibrates to the keynote of that Holy One whose ministry to man centers on healing and regeneration. In the composer's lovely music her powers of love and healing pour forth. No one can listen to it without being enfolded in a wave of its spiritual harmony. If one is conscious of its healing power, and knows it for what it is, it will add greatly to one's capacity for receiving its divine remedial benefits."[58] Duncan probably chose the *Ave Maria* not only for its restorative aspects upon her audience, but because of the healing effects it offered to her personally while she was in mourning for her children.

The familiar English translation for "Ave[59] Maria" is "Hail Mary," a salutation taken from the words of the archangel Gabriel: "Hail Mary, full of grace, the Lord is with thee; blessed are thou among women." There is little documentation for the traditional "Ave Maria" or "Hail Mary" prayer. Depending on the historical research consulted, the Ave Maria was in form as early as 538 AD. Ave Maria is also the same text for the prayer used in the recitation of the Rosary and reads: "Hail Mary, full of grace, the Lord is with thee. Blessed art thou amongst women and blessed is the fruit of thy womb, Jesus. Holy Mary, Mother of God, pray for us sinners, now, and in the hour of our death. Amen."

In 1196, the "Salutation of the Blessed Virgin" was ordered by the Bishop of Paris to be a church-ordained prayer and this salutation became commonplace, not only in Europe, but all over the world. The name Maria has been set in countless hymns and musical compositions including the song, "Maria," from Leonard Bernstein's *West Side Story*, with lyrics by Stephen Sondheim. If you listen to the lyric of "Maria"; "The most beautiful sound I have ever heard. – Say it softly and its almost like praying," – the words take on new meaning. The audience members who saw Duncan's *Ave Maria* were privileged to receive this prayer. Since we don't have the ability to see this performance today, simply by listening to the music of Bernstein, or any rendition of the *Ave Maria*, one can understand the music's ability to transform the listener, or in this case, the audience members of Duncan's *Ave Maria*, into a prayerful state.

Mary Fanton Roberts, an editor at *Arts and Decoration* magazine, and a frequent contributor to Ruth St. Denis and Ted Shawn's magazine, *Denishawn*, wrote about this transmutation: "A most potent force in Isadora's dancing is her power to evoke in her audiences a greater emotional sensitiveness to all art, toward all life in fact, sometimes as creators, sometimes as appreciators. She seems to create, as it were, audiences with a more sensitized response to beauty. It has seemed at times that she awakened in people not only the greater love for beauty, a greater humanity, but a more sympathetic understanding of what spiritual evolution meant."[60]

Journey to the Underworld

Like most mortals, Duncan she was not immune to suffering and encountered more than her share of loss; the most devastating was the deaths of her beloved children. Psychically and intuitively, Duncan received what she termed "presentiments," which informed her about their upcoming demise, a gift (or this case a curse) that she attributed to the psychological makeup of artists.

About Schubert and Duncan

Franz Schubert's music for Ave Maria was the perfect choice for Duncan. Both artists had a great deal in common. They each lived during a time of abundant creativity for the great artists. The early music of Schubert was highly emotional and individual, which is consistent with the manner in which Duncan created her dances. Both believed in their art as their religion. Schubert grew up in a strict Catholic family, went regularly to nearby church services, and was a choirboy. Yet, he "developed more and more a pantheistic religiousness stimulated by humanness and a philosophical way of thinking." (http://autria-tourism.at/personen/schubert/kirchenm6_e.html) Duncan's beliefs in pantheism were reflected in her dances, and her alignment with Nature as the source of all movement was attuned to Schubert's philosophies.

In each human being and above all in children and artists, there exists a sixth sense which enables us to divine the psychology of the soul. Two months before the deaths of my children the presentiments began. Every night on entering my studio I saw three large blackbirds flying around. I was so much troubled by the apparitions that I consulted a doctor. Before my children died, I arrived at my hotel and suddenly I saw on either side of the road quite clearly, two rows of coffins, they were not ordinary coffins, they were the coffins of children. I believe that some spirit gave a singular premonition of what was to come.[61]

Duncan attempted suicide twice during her life and, tragically, the Russian poet Sergei Esenine, whom she married, was successful in his. But, when the children died, she had reached the limits of her despair and found it difficult, if not impossible, to summon courage, or even the will to live. Traveling into the darkness is very much a part of the psychological and mystical journey. Unfortunately, our culture has no defined ritual or acceptance of navigating such soul-seeking depths, rituals that may have offered some solace.

According to her friend, Mary Fanton Roberts, "I think it would be difficult for some women who are not mothers, and even for some who are, to understand fully Isadora's love for her children. They were splendid to her, and she guarded them and watched over them and taught them the beautiful things of life in a way that was supremely touching and inspiring."[62]

The horrific circumstances of her adored children's drowning (along with their nurse) on April 19, 1913 were and are incomprehensible. The fact that Duncan's children were only beginning their lives makes this tragedy even more catastrophic. The day of the accident, "Isadora had a rehearsal; Miss Sim, (the children's Scottish nurse) and the children left in Isadora's long black car to return to

The theme of grief expressed by dancer Eleanor King. Courtesy of photographer Jane Grossenbacher.

Versailles. They had not gone far when the car stalled and the chauffeur got out to crank up the engine. He had left the car in gear, and when it leapt to a start he was unable to get back in. There were no railings along the riverbank – the heavy car rolled into the cold, swiftly flowing waters of the Seine. Attempts to free the children and their governess were useless; the current was too strong, and by the time the car was located it was too late."[63] Duncan was devastated.

After the children's deaths, Roberts remembered spending an afternoon with Isadora and noticed that "something of her [Duncan's] own existence seemed to have vanished with them." Sitting in the room that was filled with memories was a magnificent Eugene Carriere painting, depicting "a mother gathering to her breast the spirits of her lost children. Isadora cherished this picture more than any possession she had, and I used to think at times she felt her own children were in the room with her, and that the spirits of her little babies had come back to console her in those terrible days."[64]

She spent weeks staring at the walls and "entered a dreary land of grayness where no will to live or move existed. When real sorrow is encountered there is for the stricken, no gesture, no expression. Like Niobe turned to stone, I sat and longed for annihilation in death."[65] Tormented with the voices of her children, she lived with constant agony. Several years later in a cruel twist of fate, Duncan received what she thought was her personal trunk by messenger, and upon opening it up, she was shocked to view the clothing of her deceased children.

> I found it [the trunk] contained the clothes of Deirdre and Patrick. When I saw them there, before my eyes once more – the little dresses they had last worn – the coats and the little caps – I heard again that cry which I had heard when I saw them lying dead – a strange, long, wailing cry, which I did not

"After Eugene Carriere," created by artist, Kelly Borsheim after viewing an exhibit of Carriere's work. Carriere was one of Duncan's favorite artists.

recognize as my own voice – but if some cruelly-hurt animal called its death-cry from my throat.[66]

The words she chose to describe her acceptance of their deaths *immediately* after the accident are words of enormous power and strength, reflecting a similar acceptance and strength that the Virgin Mary is depicted showing when her son died.

"They [her friends] feared the shock would make me insane, but I was, at that time, lifted into a state of exaltation. I saw everyone around me weeping, but I did not weep. On the contrary, I felt the immense desire to console everyone else. Looking back it was difficult for me to understand my strange state of mind. Was it that I was really in a state of clairvoyance, and that I knew that death does not exist – that those two little cold images of wax were not my children, but merely their cast-off garments – That the souls of my children lived in radiance, but lived for ever."[67] Duncan's ideas about life after death, in which the soul lives forever, echoed metaphysical principles, and no doubt the idea of her children's souls living forever must have given her great comfort.[68]

Her friend, the actress Cécile Sorel, described the funeral procession. "Alone, Isadora walked at the head of the endless cortege. She resembled a mourner of ancient times. The people were crossing themselves as they followed the folds of her dress. I wanted to kiss her naked feet in their sandals."[69] During her time of grief, Duncan writes that she "entered into a phase of intense mysticism. I felt that my children's spirits hovered near me – that they would return to console me on earth."[70] In addition to Duncan's psychic abilities, after the deaths of Deirdre and Patrick, she described a vision, or a resurrection, of the children on earth in which she encounters them while walking along a beach during a gray, autumn afternoon. "I was walking alone along the sands when, suddenly, I saw going just ahead of me the figures of my children Deirdre and Patrick, hand in hand. I

When the American poet Witter Bynner saw Isadora perform Ave Maria *in New York, he wrote:*

Isadora (To Her Six Dancers)

*Beauty came out of the early
    world,
Her hyacinthine hair still
    curled,
her robe still white on auroral
    limbs;
And her body sang the self-
    same hymns
It long ago had sung to the
    morn
When death gave birth and
    love was born.
And once again her presence
    proved,
As most immortally she moved,
That in her meditative eye
The child of death can never
    die
But dances with inspired feet
On every hill, in every street.
She raised her hand – and
    Irma came,
Theresa, Lisel, each like a
    flame,
Anna, Erica, Gretel: the
    thread
Of life still dying, never dead
And like a bird-song in a
    wood,
Within their very heart she
    stood.*
    – POTD, 84.

called to them but they ran laughing ahead of me just out of reach. I ran after them – followed – called – and suddenly they disappeared in the midst of the sea-spray."[71]

Dancing Again

On November 24, 1914, over a year after her children's deaths, Duncan returned to the United States after turning over her palatial French estate to Les Dames de France for use as a hospital center for the Allied who were wounded during the war. Witnessing her school of creative art turned into a hospital filled with dying soldiers was yet another reminder of her grief. "My Temple of Art was turned into a Calvary of Martyrdom and, in the end, into a charnel house of bloody wounds and death. Where I had thought of strains of heavenly music, there were only raucous cries of pain."

Isadora had previously sent her students, "the Duncanettes" or the "Isadorables," to New York, extending her school to her homeland. Privately, she hoped that she would be able to enlist the aid of the American government to help her sponsor her vision for a school. She premiered *Ave Maria* in New York City at Carnegie Hall on December 3, 1914, but curiously she never mentions the piece in her autobiography, even though it was a powerful work and considered one of her greatest.

Ave Maria consisted of two versions; one was a solo for herself, and in the other version she performed with her students in a group. *Ave Maria* was her prayer and an intimate encounter with the spiritual dimensions of life.

In the group version, each girl moves ahead, her chest forward. The arms are flung wide and then closed above the head, the wrists crossing, like the beating of great angelic wings. The action is so simple and subdued that when, in the third verse of the song, each dancer suddenly brings her knee up in a skip, it comes like a sudden release or uprushing of the spirit. The body and the arms make gestures of adoration and humility toward the Virgin and the Child, but the movements are so strong that the humility seems only tender, not self-abasing. At the end, the feet move very rapidly and smoothly, though the angels move on half-toe, not en pointe, while the arms rise slowly upwards. There is nothing indecisive or sentimental about these gestures – they are Michelangelesque and immense. The Virgin Mary shrinks back, as if from the Angel of Annunciation, then makes imploring gestures with her hands and arms. Then, though her head is bending low over the Child, her arms, wrists, and hands move backwards in a gesture of surprise. The angels' arm movements in the dance encompass the earth, reach to the sky, and come from the heart in yearning, as the dancers offer themselves to the Virgin and the Child.[72]

Mixed Reviews

Duncan also performed *Ave Maria* when she was living in Russia in November 1923. She arranged for a private party and invited Leonard Borisovich Krasin, a devoted fan and head of the Soviet Trade Commission, to attend. She decided to dance *Ave Maria* for him. "I'll make him sit on the sofa with the golden swans and dance that piece for him."[73] The moment the music began, a radiant Madonna appeared. The Russian composer, Benediktov, however, was critical. He asked Ilya Ilyich Scheider, her manager and companion while she was in Russia, "Is this Duncan? Why, the whole thing's nothing but an immense fraud! There's nothing there." Schneider relayed the message to Duncan to spare her the embarrassment of hearing Benediktov tell her in person, as he proclaimed he would. Duncan replied, "He mustn't come here again. It is important that I am surrounded only by friends and people who understand me."[74]

Six months after the performance in New York, John Collier wrote a review in *Survey* magazine, but he never

Lori Belilove photographed by © Margaretta Mitchell.
Courtesy of the Isadora Duncan Dance Foundation.

mentioned Duncan dancing solo. "Here was the breath of God, yes, the beatific vision was in three little ordinary human souls."[75] It's unclear in the reviews whether Duncan performed with the group in *Ave Maria* as a soloist or danced the piece alone. The following year in New York, she included readings from the Psalms and the Beatitudes in her performance,[76] and the theatre took on an almost holy atmosphere. It was a meaningful departure for Duncan, who had disdain for traditional religion, to read passages from the Bible during the concert. Poignantly, she read the words: "Blessed are they that mourn for they shall be comforted. They that sow in tears shall reap in joy." After she danced *Ave Maria* she read: "Praise ye the Lord. Praise him, all his angels, let everything that hath breath praise the Lord."[77] Did she find comfort in those words? Her identification with God during a period of intense suffering and mourning was surprising, not so much that she would turn to the Bible for comfort, but that she would choose to publicly share her liturgical leanings with her audience.

One reviewer from the *Boston Transcript* who attended the performance was not impressed and complained in his review, "Her performances are sicklied over now with the pale cast of some very immature and hasty thought…It is a most disheartening and amateurish mixture of music and recited literature, from the Bible and other sources equally unsuited to any such purpose."[78] *The New York Times* wrote a review under the headline, "Symphony Aids Dancers: Isadora Duncan's Pupils Appear with New York Orchestra." However, *Ave Maria* appeared as a mere mention in the critic's review.

In 1916, she performed *Ave Maria* as a soloist at the Metropolitan Opera House. Irma Duncan, one of the "Isadorables" who danced on the program, described it in her memoirs: "The program had a religious character, it opened with a requiem march and Isadora's presentation of Schubert's *Ave Maria*. Isadora's magnetism has not diminished with the year, but her older pupils did most of the dancing."[79] Although the work is only cited in a newspaper article of unknown origin, her ability to capture the attention of the audience was apparent.

A critic for this 1916 performance wrote: "The Metropolitan, usually given over to a hiatus of darkness and quiet on Tuesday evenings, was crowded to the many doors last night with an audience to honor and behold the dancing of Isadora Duncan. The performer, unaided this time by her troupe of young girls, held the thousands of eyes riveted upon her every beautiful gesture and incited a clapping of the thousands of hands, which during every dance had to clinch in a stemming of emotions."[80] The critic continued to describe the rest of the program and although he/she never wrote about *Ave Maria* in detail, it is the first time that Duncan performed *Ave Maria* in tandem with another work. The words penned by this critic capture the electric energies that must have been flowing through the theatre that evening. While his words are a passionate description of *Symphonic Fragment of the Redemption,* they are worth noting, as they provide an authentic and intimate background for the introduction of *Ave Maria*. They also transport the reader into the audience that evening.

Miss Duncan was discovered upon the deep shadowed stage, utterly prostrate, her white robes draped down upon her huddled figure as upon a thing grotesquely useless and inert. Then slowly, laboriously, the stir of life came; one could see it only in the trembling fingers at first, then along the uplifting arms. Then to the knees, then to full height — and the figure could stride and assert itself in broad deliberate motion. It was all a cycle of slow gestures, unalterably slow and stern, early inward impulse of it seeming to find flight and oppression from the unseen forces without. And when, in the end, self-mastery came, with head high and face gladdened with the pride of peace, it was as if a great battle of

Preparing for a Performance

"While filling her engagement, Isadora Duncan devoted all of her thought to her work. She would always lie in bed for two hours before going to the theatre. Then her maids would give her a full body massage, wrap her in blankets and carry her to a cab. She remained blanketed to keep her muscles warm until her appearance, and after her appearance she would go straight to her hotel. She would see or talk to nobody after the final curtain."– Alexis Kosloff, *close friend and dancer with the Imperial Russian Ballet, "Personal Glimpses,"* The Literary Digest, *October 8, 1927, in ID, 52.*

humanity unlimited has been enacted through one strong, transparent soul. Certainly for sense of continuity as well as for wealth of beauty this number which went on into Schubert's *Ave Maria* was the vastest of the evening."[81]

A Target

It is often the case that artists, particularly artists who attempt to challenge the status quo are ample targets for the press, and Duncan was no exception. The American press in particular frequently wrote about her "art" at her expense. In 1903 Ernest Haskell, a critic for the *New York Dramatic Mirror*, didn't think that her work meant much until she traveled to Europe and became the rage there. In his review, he wrote a particularly funny piece that had more to say about human nature than the nature of Isadora's dancing. He didn't see "why a woman standing on one leg with her eyes rolled up meant anything, but a stork, and she wasn't a pretty woman, and I thought it was in bad taste."[82]

> She was beautiful when she struck a pose, but awful when she moved. New York failed to see anything in the idea of a dance expressing the meaning of a poem. A clog, a high kick or a cake walk was our limit. Then, Isadora, the lean and lovely one went to London and dances in the drawing rooms, those meccas through which Americans who can't make good on this side seem to become prophets! The trouble with us over here is that we are too ready to break into cheerful smiles over things that we do not comprehend. Once someone tells us about it we go to it like sheep to worship, but we'll flock the other way more quickly unless we get a hint from some foreign source. [83]

Even after her tragic death in an automobile accident, when her famous long flowing scarf became entangled in the wheels of her car, some of her critics had no shame. In a small picture in an unnamed magazine, a caption read "Psychoneurotic Women of Genius," with the following text: "Isadora Duncan, renowned American dancer, was admired throughout the world for her creative ideas and graceful artistry, but estranged her native public through her psychoneurotic eccentricities." It's not clear what those "psychoneurotic" tendencies are because the editor never reveals any further text. Yet, the photo appearing above the caption is of a woman at the turn of the century who doesn't resemble Duncan at all. It is hard to believe that editors of this unnamed magazine would knowingly publish the wrong photograph of one of the most famous dancers of her time.

Oddly enough, her choreography was termed "psycho-choreographic" by the French sculptor George Gray Barnard, who was asked by the French government to create a statue of her likeness. He defined the term "psycho-choreographic" as meaning "to visualize by poetry of motion, a series of abstract emotions so that they will convey meaning to the consciousness of the observer…She is the Light of tomorrow a torch that lights the path of progress, socially, spiritually, altruistically."[84]

A Woman of Courage

Duncan was unconvention defined. She never seemed to care what her critics said, for she seemed to follow her own internal prompting and vision for the sacred in dance. This philosophy was apparent when she was offered a large sum of money to dance in Berlin and the promoters told her that she would be billed as the "First Barefoot Dancer."

Duncan was not ashamed of her body in any respect, and even when she was pregnant with Patrick, her son by her then lover, Paris Singer, she still performed although her "condition" was obvious to her audiences. Duncan explained to one audience member, "That was just what she meant by dancing to express Love – Woman – Formation. Botticelli's picture, you know." She said, "The fruitful Earth

Isadora Speaks

I have come to bring about a great renaissance of religion through the dance, to bring the knowledge of the beauty and holiness of the human body, through its expressions of movement and not to dance for the amusement of the overfed bourgeois. I am seeking something you don't understand. – Con O'Leary, T.P.'s Weekly for June 2, 1928, in ID.

– the three Graces enciente – the Madonna. That is what my Dance means."[85] The image of the Madonna as full, ripe, and ready to give birth is a powerful image, and the fact that Duncan felt a kinship with the image of the Madonna provides some clue as to her impetus for making the *Ave Maria*, years after Patrick's birth.

In 1921, Duncan moved to Soviet Russia to begin the dance school that she had dreamed of, and the Duncan dancers debuted at the Bolshoi Theatre on the "occasion of a gala celebrating the anniversary of the revolution, and chose to dance *Ave Maria*." [86] "All along, it was obvious that she was, as she said herself, a "revolutionist" and not a Bolshevik and that her attacks on formal religion in no way voided her passionate beliefs in the soul. Anyone who would dance *Ave Maria* at an official communist celebration was patently neither a Bolshevik not a destroyer of spiritual expression."[87] Three thousand people attended the performance and the theatre was packed from wall to wall. Even Lenin attended the concert. At the end he was described as "applauding, crying in a loud voice, 'Bravo, bravo, Miss Duncan.'"[88]

Ave Maria was so important to her that she selected it for her last appearance on the stage during her engagement at the Théâtre Mogador in Paris on July 8, 1927, with the Pasdeloup Orchestra under the direction of a prominent conductor of that time, Albert Wolff. She was fifty years old, and gossip was rampant that she could no longer dance due to the fact that her initial selections for the program were short. In an effort to quell the gossip, Duncan added some pieces. Among the new selections was *Ave Maria*. Duncan was not only annoyed by the gossip, but by the fact that the additions never made it to the evening program because of lack of funds to redo the printing. She could not have been too concerned with the elements of rehearsal in the usual sense of preparing her body, for the day before the concert, she went to the theatre for a dress rehearsal with Victor Seroff, her friend and one of her biographers. He explained:

Not many ever witnessed her rehearsals, which indeed were unusual. She went down to greet Albert Wolff, who was standing at the conductor's desk waiting for her to begin. The orchestra was about to clear a space for her, but Isadora shook her head and told them it would not be necessary – all she needed, she said, would be a chair placed near the first violins and the conductor's desk. Whispering to Wolff, she asked him to play Franck's *Redemption*, and without taking off her cape or hat, she remained immobile in her chair listening to the music. In fact, after the orchestra finished playing the composition, Isadora sat motionless in the silent theater, while Wolff waited for her further requests. Then Isadora walked up to him, bowed graciously to the orchestra – and that was the end of dress rehearsal."[89]

Because management did such a poor job in public relations, the theatre was far from full, but "distinguished members of the artistic world and Isadora's faithful old admirers made an enthusiastic audience nonetheless."[90] Gilson MacCormack, a reviewer, wrote in the August issue of the *Dancing Times* of London: "I feel that one great mistake of Miss Duncan's is her choice of music to interpret – but the sight of a woman clad in a Greek tunic and purple scarf alternately lifting her arms aloft and then brandishing her fists at the audience is a sight fit to provoke mirth for a long time to come."[91] When she danced *Liebestod,* he was less than kind, writing, "We all know how painful it is to watch this scene sung by an over-ripe prima donna. At all events, we have the consolation of being able to close our eyes without losing anything by so doing. I regret to say I found myself compelled to adopt the same procedure during Miss Duncan's miming of the scene, even though she did not sing it."[92] However, MacCormack must have opened his eyes when Isadora danced *Ave Maria,* because he ended the review with an interesting line considering that he was a music critic, as was the fashion during that time, since dance reviewers were all but unknown: "If Pavlova's weakness lies in the banality of her choice of music, the fault of Isadora Duncan is to choose that which is beyond physical expression."[93] It is not clear what he meant by "beyond physical expression." Perhaps the sacredness of the piece defied physical embodiment in his mind. Or, the subject matter of the work was simply irritating to him.

MacCormack's opinions were in the minority, especially in regards to *Ave Maria*, when Duncan "with maternal arms lulling an imaginary babe, was so personal and heartrending in its simplicity that it provoked unashamed sobs throughout the audience. At the end of the performance she was cheered and called back to the stage again."[94] Although Duncan had performed *Ave Maria* in the years since its premiere, it was not a piece that she did constantly. No doubt the subject matter of mother and child (Madonna and child) was quite painful for her, because when she performed this piece, she was completely enveloped by it. Dancing *Ave Maria* must certainly have resurrected her grief, and she surely was not seeking to "mime" her feelings. Ten years later she created *Mother*, another hauntingly beautiful work.

After the concert, her last stage performance, she spent the next two days resting, and according to Seroff was compelled to speak about her thoughts about it:

For the first time I have achieved something I have been striving to do all my life. I am not sure I can explain it in words. Ever since I watched Ellen Terry's and Duse's acting, I learned that the true expression of tragedy lies, not in the actress's raging on the stage, or harassing the audience with wild screams, but, on the contrary, in remaining absolutely mute and immobile when stunned by a sudden blow of fate. I understood that a long time

Isadora Speaks

One of the grossest misconceptions is the idea that a shock of pain, or deep grief, should be shown by the hand clutching the heart. "What does the heart have to do with it?" It may suddenly beat faster, but actual pain, physical pain, your heart does not feel. Pain strikes you in the stomach, or even lower – that is where it hurts. How many in an audience would understand that gesture, since they expect you to clutch your heart? In fact, I hate to think what interpretation they are apt to give to my way of indicating sudden, grief, physical pain.
– TRI, 425.

ago, but how to have the audience too feel it in the same way that the actress does? How to make the audience stop breathing? Yes, to have your audience remain breathless as long as you yourself remain on the stage mute and immobile. That is true art, and I believe at that matinee I achieved it for the first time.[95]

The Duncan Legacy

Isadora Duncan's contributions to the current forms of modern dance were enormous and her choreographic and philosophical offerings have survived over the decades even though many dancers/choreographers are reluctant to give her full credit for her impact on their own work. For instance, Mark Morris, one of the best choreographers working today, was eager to credit Duncan for her boon to the feminists. When he was asked in an interview about Duncan's influence on his masterpiece, *L'Allegro il Penseroso ed il Moderato*, (which I believe contained a significant Duncanesque style of movement), he was quick to dismiss her as little more than a "barefoot dancer." "I think that it [Duncan's influence] is the same effect that Blake had on my work. Who has ever seen a Duncan work? I have seen beautiful reconstructions. But the fact is that aside from coming from the Orientalist school and the Denishawn school with barefoot dancing, esthetic dancing from the turn of the century was inseparable from feminism. It was like in 'The Music Man,' the Grecian urn number when Hermione Gingold does barefoot dancing. It's very funny, but it's a comment on that period of early feminism and mysticism and taking off your corset and shoes. That was the biggest thing about it. She was a big woman who was barefoot and danced without a girdle and underpants."[96]

George Balanchine, perhaps the greatest choreographer of any time, recognized the value of studying statues to examine the lines of the body for creating form in his ballets, just as Duncan was interested in studying the lines of

the Greco-Roman sculptures for inspiration for her movements. According to Lincoln Kirstein, General Director for the New York City Ballet, Balanchine's "acrobatic divertissement for the 'Victory' dance in *Aïda* and the *danse du ventre* for the priestesses in the same opera were based on religious sculptures. For the *Bacchanale* in Tannhäuser, Balanchine acquainted himself with Isadora Duncan's experience."[97]

An amusing story of Duncan's influence occurred when Kirstein, who was a one-day only coordinator for the Dance Project in 1937, outlined his ideas for a program called *The History of American Dance*. He told modern dance legend Helen Tamiris, "You, Miss Tamaris will dance Isadora Duncan." To which Tamiris replied, "And who, Mr. Kirstein, will dance Tamaris?"

Synchronistically, as much as Duncan despised in "ballet" the unnatural techniques required to perform, the lives of both Duncan and ballet would extend years after her death. In 1934, the School of American Ballet (home of New York City Ballet) rented space in a loft building where "Isadora once had her studio, paid for by Paris Singer. One iron post *stood stubbornly* in the center of a splendid open space, but it could not be removed without the collapse of the entire three upper floors. This column assumed an extraordinary metaphorical importance; its implacable challenge to our whole future seemed to be magnetized, in its formidable uprightness and slim mineral solidity; as every possible negative threat."[98] The irony that her former studio was utilized as a ballet practice-space would have made her skin crawl. However, she would no doubt have enjoyed the fact that the iron post (symbolizing her iron will) could not be removed.

Duncan would not have appreciated the critical thoughts of the young Balanchine who, after witnessing her performance in Russia (as a young boy), offered his description: "To me it was absolutely unbelievable – a drunken, fat woman who for hours was rolling around like a pig. It was

Lori Belilove photographed by © Margaretta Mitchell.
Courtesy of the Isadora Duncan Dance Foundation.

the most awful thing."[99] However, his thoughts were in the minority. When she performed at the Lewisohn Stadium in New York, dancer Helen Tamiris was there. She described Duncan's ability to hold her audiences spellbound: "She started on the ground, lying close to the floor and – it took a long time – the only physical action was the very slow movement which carried her from prone to erect with arms outstretched. At the finish, everyone was crying and I was crying, too." [100]

Technique

Duncan's use of natural and simple movements such as running, skipping, leaping, and walking may not seem like a difficult method to learn, however she also employed barre work to develop strength and suppleness of the dancer's bodies. Although Duncan often spoke about her hatred of ballet, it seems very likely that she studied ballet in depth at some point in her life because she developed a consistent and well-thought-out barre for her dancers much like the barre that ballet dancers today use as part of their daily practice. While Duncan's exercises differ from traditional ballet exercises, she utilized a similar technique in terms of ballet positions. The difference in her barre was that the weight of the body was quite different and the energetic stance required by the dancers was not as rigid as traditional ballet.

> Sometimes, the feet were kicked over the head in front, sideways and backwards. The knees were turned out for sidekicks, the leg was held straight, and the toes were pointed. In other exercises at the barre the knees were bent outward until the dancer sat on her heels; she then raised herself on her toes and sank slowly, holding her spine straight. She also used "Tanagra figures," a series of movements derived from Greek art, for training her pupils in the basic vocabulary of her dance.[101]

Duncan's dances radiate from joyful and melodious forms of movement to deeper, darker, and more moving choreography containing a universal element. This element is fundamental to her philosophy of the dance; that is, to dance with the truth of the body. Her spontaneity, emotional richness, and articulate understanding of the music provided for this truth in dance style. According to Julia Levien, one of the early Duncan dancers, "The essentials of the Duncan approach is in finding the original impulses of motives relating to motion. All movements must start at the center, Isadora taught. That center is correlated physically to the solar plexus. Anatomically, it is the muscle belt of the diaphragm that controls the breath and reacts by both expanding and contracting negatively according to the variety of emotions imposed on it. From this awareness, Duncan developed a rational sense of primal body movement as well as arm and hand gestures that radiate from an inner core of energy, liberating the disciplined body into a cycle of renewed and wave-like energy. The movement that starts from within emanated from the center outward for infinite renewal. Music supplies the emotional springboard for this."[102]

One of the few reviewers who recognized the center or solar plexus as the region where Duncan's movements originated was Mabel Dodge Luhan. In 1915, after she attended a Duncan concert in New York, Luhan wrote, "Power arose in her from her Center and flowed vividly along her limbs before our eyes in living beauty and delight."[103] Luhan was an ardent Duncan supporter and when she visited New York along with other "radicals," she set up meetings with local politicians to help her raise monies for her school. Because of Duncan's less than idyllic behavior during those meetings, the fundraising was insufficient, and Duncan consequently opened up her schools out of the country. The natural friendship between the two is understandable however, since they were both highly intelligent, studied metaphysics and psychology, and shared an interest in the archetypal feminine.

Although Duncan's artistry has been dismissed by many critics assuming that she had no technique, that is a false claim. Andre Levinson wrote about her at length, and although he "deplored her iconoclasm, with its admixture of self-congratulation," thought she was "a bad influence," and that her "ideas were all wrong," he also wrote that "the flame that burned within this exceptional being lit them up, for a time, with splendor."[104] According to one of the six "Isadorables," Marie-Theresa, when a student asked her to teach her "Duncan's walk" in a day, she replied with anger, "A day!!! It has taken me years to learn how to walk properly."[105]

The Cosmic Axis

Duncan's technique arose not only from her great understanding of her own body, but what author Nicholas Whitehead terms the "Cosmic Axis." There are three elements of the Cosmic Axis which directly align with Duncan's technique. Whitehead believed that the "Axis is a vertical channel which joins, transfixes, and binds the Worlds. It is thus symbolically, the 'spindle' of creation around which the whole cosmic order revolves."[106]

When Whitehead speaks of the "joining, transfixing and binding of the Worlds," he is referring to the world of form (the earth) and the world of spirit (heaven). Certainly, Duncan was able to link the worlds of spirit and form through her dancing. The second point that Whitehead makes is that the Axis can also function as a "via sancta" or a holy way that provides for the initiate's passage between those two worlds. Duncan's dancing in form was the "via sancta" and gave her the opportunity to navigate those worlds while she was lost in her dancing. Whitehead's third point is that the Axis functions as a conduit through which spiritual energies may flow between the worlds. The spiritual energies flowing through Duncan when she danced originated in her theory of the solar plexus as initiator of her movements. This Axis is written about in the mystical writings of the Kabbalah, which were part of the Rosicrucian studies that Duncan's lover Gordon Craig studied in London.

In the Kabbalistic study, the trinity of body, mind and spirit are called Jechidah, Chiah, and Neschamah and "it is impossible to conceive of one of them without the other two. The Jechidah or 'Divine Spark' contains the belief of 'that in me which is more than me myself', the deepest layer of consciousness. It corresponds with the Crown (also the Crown chakra in Eastern mysticism.) The Chiah, or 'essential will' is the creative impulse of the Jechidah, through which one obtains self-realization. It corresponds with Wisdom. The Neschamah corresponds with the Great Mother, or Understanding of self."[107] Duncan was able to utilize this trinity of body, mind and spirit through her choreographic works. She used her "divine spark" as her creative impulse and that impulse is apparent in her understanding of the significance of the Mother in *Ave Maria* and other dances.

The center (of the body) is called Tipheretch and represents the Axis. Did Duncan realize how her philosophies were in tandem with the metaphysical principles of the Golden Dawn and the Kabbalah? We will never know for sure. It is revelatory, however, that she chose to title one of her essays on dance, "The Philosopher's Stone of Dancing." Because "The Philosopher's Stone" is a direct reference to alchemy, one wonders what her exposure and thoughts on alchemy actually were. In this essay she wrote about three forms of dancers: "Dancers who consider dance as a 'gymnastic drill,' dancers who command their bodies to perform a type of 'remembered feeling,' and the third, those who convert the body into a luminous fluidity, surrendering it to the inspiration of the soul. This third sort of dancer understands that the body, by force of the soul, can in fact be converted to a luminous fluid. The flesh becomes light and transparent, as shown through the X-ray – but with the difference that the human soul is lighter than these rays. When, in its divine power, it completely possesses the body, it converts that into a luminous moving cloud and thus can manifest itself in the whole of its divinity."[108] Duncan was certainly no stranger to alchemical philosophy in thought and form.

The Chakras

It is fascinating to explore Duncan's ideas from the perspective of chakra study (*see* The Healing Aspects of Dance, in Chapter 1). The third chakra, or the solar plexus portion of the body, is the energy center most relevant to Duncan's philosophy of the dance. The color that the third chakra is said to manifest is yellow. Yellow is considered the "Wisdom of the Spirit, and the color is the symbol of Air vibrating between Earth and Heaven and carrying the messages of the Father to man on Earth."[109] In Christian symbology, yellow is the emblem of the sun, signifying divinity. The third chakra is concerned with thought and intellect, and it is also the center where psychic messages can be received. Because of her psychic and intuitive powers, Duncan was probably an able messenger between the worlds of earth and heaven.

What is also noteworthy is that the third chakra is responsible for "filtering spiritual information and that passing on of information is what keeps the bodily aspects of the body/spirit connection strong and healthy. A very open third chakra in an otherwise healthy and aligned chakra system is a sign that the spirit and body are communicating. This third chakra is gathering energy and information in order to make the leap in the conscious aspects of thought."[110]

Whether Duncan was privy to an in-depth study of the chakras is unclear, but it is possible that in her conversations with Craig, who had studied metaphysical principles, they discussed these ideas. She writes in *Fragments and Thoughts*[111] that it was a mistake to call her a dancer: "I am the magnetic center[112] to convey the emotional expression of the orchestra. From my soul sprang fiery rays to connect me." Duncan understood the interaction between the metaphysical principles of color and light, and although she

Isadora Duncan Study by Abraham Walkowitz. Pastel on red paper. n.d.(ca. 1917) . Courtesy of University Gallery, University of Delaware. Gift of Virginia Zabriskie.

doesn't mention the chakras by name, her knowledge about the solar plexus parallels much of the literature of the third chakra.

Her description of the solar plexus as "center" and its effects on her work, is not only visionary, but also distinguishes her as a metaphysical scholar:

I sought the source of spiritual expression to flow into the channels of the body filling it with vibrating light – the centrifugal force reflecting the spirit's vision. After many months, when I had learned to concentrate all my force into this one Center I found that thereafter, when I listened to music the rays and vibrations of the music streamed into this one fount of light within me – there they reflected themselves in Spiritual Vision, not the brain's mirror; but the soul's, and from this vision I could express them in dance. I have often tried to express to artists this first basic theory of my Art.[113]

Body and Soul

The spiritual expression that Duncan accessed no doubt offered her moments of unrestrained ecstasy, and she frequently mentions these "other worldly" experiences in her writings. She contacted "the other world" not only in her dancing, but in her philosophical study. What is most unusual is that these profound observations about the spiritual meanings in her dances are not discussed by most dance historians from a spiritual standpoint. If one reflects upon some of her statements in her books, it seems inexcusable that Duncan's importance as a spiritual philosopher is not mentioned. "This extraordinary spirit, or as the Germans called it *geist*, of the feeling of Holiness, *der Heiligthum des Gedankes*, (the holiness of thought), that I met, made me often feel as if I had been introduced into a world of superior and Godlike thinkers."[114] When she describes the hours she spent with the man she called her "Archangel," who played the piano while she danced, her words read like the description of a mystical experience.

And in the studio our two arts blended into one in a marvelous manner, while under his influence my dance became etherealized. There spent holy hours, our united souls borne up by the mysterious force which possessed us. Often as I danced and he played, as I lifted my arms and my soul went up from my body in the long flight. It seemed as if we had created a spiritual entity quite apart from ourselves, and, as sound and gesture flowed up to the Infinite, another answer echoed from above. I believe that from the psychic force of this musical moment, when our two spirits were so attuned in the holy energy of love, we were on the verge of another world.[115]

Isadora's "Archangel" was a thirty-one-year-old musician named Walter Rummel, who filled the void of emptiness in her life although he rejected her sexual interests. He preferred instead to "make love to himself behind the closed doors of his room,"[116] rather than to her, lying frustrated in the bedroom. Duncan was no doubt shattered by this affront.

Duncan's understanding of the metaphysical and theological principles of spirit manifested in the body are only some of her deep contributions to the dance. Her evolved consciousness – which led her to call for woman's complete ownership of her own body – were quite advanced in a pre-feminist era. Her lover Gordon Craig left perhaps one of the best descriptions of Duncan's originality and magic – a legacy which endures today.

I have something to say about Isadora Duncan. In fact, I have a good deal to say of her. People called her a great artist – a Greek goddess – but she was nothing of the kind. She was something quite different from anyone and anything else. What more she had, no one will ever describe. She was a forerunner. All she did was done with great ease – or so it seemed, at least.

This it was which gave her an appearance of power. She projected the dance into this world of ours in full belief that what she was doing was right and great. And it was. She threw away ballet skirts and ballet thoughts. She discarded shoes and stockings too. She put on bits of stuff which when hung up on a peg looked more like torn rags than anything else; when she put them on they became transformed. She transformed them into marvels of beauty and at every step she took they spoke. I do not exaggerate.

She was speaking her own language (do you understand? Her own language: Have you got it?) not echoing any ballet master, and so she came to move as no one has ever seen anyone move before...How is it that we know that she is speaking her own language? We know it, for we see her head, her hands, gently active, as are her feet, her whole person. And if she is speaking, what is she saying? No one would be able to report truly (or exactly – extraordinary, isn't it), yet no one present has a moment's doubt. Only this can we say – that she was telling to the air the very things we longed to hear and until she came we had never dreamed we should hear; and now we heard them, and this sent us all into an unusual state of joy, and I sat still and speechless.[117]

Ruth St. Denis in an exquisite studio portrait, "The Study of the Madonna."
Courtesy of The Ruth St. Denis Foundation.

Chapter 3

Ruth St. Denis

Capricorn, Born January 20, 1878

The ruler of Capricorn is Saturn. This wonderful Cosmos is one harmonious whole, and all its activities are rhythmic, and have been so since time began. Although Saturn belongs to a past generation he still continues to reign. This is not an easy type to analyze, but two main elements are always to be found in connection with its highest manifestation of humanity, namely noble ambition, and an extraordinary power of adaptability to environment. Their enthusiasm is of the kind that grows and gathers force through coming in touch with the enthusiasm of the masses of their fellow men and women, and they throw themselves into the task of guiding a popular movement – to a successful issue; winning great praise and much esteem by their ability.

The religious life of the advanced Capricornian is the strongest and the most important element, for ambition when it comes to its height is transmuted into aspiration, and this type is peculiarly suited to the office of the priesstesshood. The handing on of tradition, the right and reverent rendering of ritual and the dutiful observance of all kinds of things ceremonial are thoroughly congenial to the daughter of Saturn. She also holds very strong convictions as to the value of all outward and visible signs of inward and spiritual grace, insisting on the reverent posture, and the methodical use of set forms of praise and prayer. The fact that these forms are antiquated and no longer understood by the majority of the people, in no way detracts from their value in her eyes. They belong to a great past and are therefore venerable.

Rhythmic chanting or repetition of invocation and praise does calm the physical body and steady the mind and attune the soul, thus preparing the whole man to respond fully and freely to the vibrations of the higher plane. It is part of the priestesses duty to know how and when to use this special key to that wonderful Kingdom of Heaven – the Spiritual Universe – which is within and around us all. The endeavor to establish the laws of the Kingdom of Heaven upon earth is the aim of every true daughter of this sign when she has attained to its heights.[1]

Ruth Dennis[2] was born in Newark, New Jersey, on a farm. "I grew up poor. My mother had an MD degree from the University of Michigan and my father was an inventor who sent up the first balloon in New Jersey. My mother took in boarders to make ends meet, and most of the talk was on politics and things of the spirit."[3] Her first dancing experience was at the age of three when her father took her to a barn dance, where he played the fiddle, and as soon as she heard the music, she "began to jounce up and down, and Father, seizing a tambourine from the trap drummer, thrust it into my hands. I started beating out time, with some uncertain footwork."[4] Both of her parents possessed both creativity and high intelligence and although her mother would play a pivotal role throughout her life, her father's influence was also important.

Her mother, who she has credited as "so truly great a person that I cannot even attempt to do her justice – she was about fifty years ahead of her time. She sensed life in an infinitely more intense way than any of the people in our neighborhood."[5] When Ruth was a child, her mother would read aloud to her from the Bible, omitting the section on Jesus's death in an effort to spare the impressionable and sensitive young girl. When Ruth read the New Testament to herself, alone, it had a tremendous impact, informing her lifelong quest for linking the spiritual component with her dances. Her identification with Jesus was so strong that she hid in the family's barn recreating herself in his image.

> I took two long bath towels from the linen closet upstairs, and hid them in my room. I went out into the barn and began to shape two wooden boards to fit my feet and contrived straps of tape and cord to hold them on. I took these belongings up to the old north bedroom where I would not be disturbed. I, who was generally so open in all my doings, felt an irresistible need to be as secretive as possible. Intuitively, I knew that this outward expression of a sudden and mystical identification with Christ would only look ridiculous to a loving family. I was performing something very close to a sacred ritual as I hung the bath towels around my body, fastening them at my shoulders and waist by cords, and put the wooden sandals on my feet. Then, I stood in a kind of daze, staring at myself for a long time in the mirror which I had taken off the wall and stood upon a chair. For that moment, I really believed myself the little Jesus, and a curious flame burned in me that, in the light of the later wisdom, can only be interpreted as a faint by intense identification with a cosmic consciousness. I had touched a Divine spark.[6]

Her personal alignment with the spiritual forces both within and outside of her, led St. Denis like Duncan, to discover great joy in movement. She explored the woods and hills on the farm, and enacted her own ritual while watching the sun fade in the evenings. "I made a funny little bow, almost dropping to my knees. No one taught me to do this, I simply obeyed an impulse to honor the sun." [7] A born ritualist, believing that "everything has to have meaning," Ruth's philosophy that "dance began in the unconscious, not in the body," was based in personal revelations of her own body. "I believe that we should regard the dance fundamentally as a Life experience, as the ultimate means of expression and is not something to be taken on from the outside – something to be painfully learned – or something to be imitated. Artificial and limited ideas of the dance have done cruel and grotesque things to its servants, as, indeed they have to most artists of the stage."[8]

Such "grotesque things" included her limited exposure to ballet classes. After three weeks of instruction, her teacher, suggested that she enroll in another class, because, "I was clumsy and asked inconvenient questions." She studied briefly at the famous evangelist, Dwight L. Moody's seminary, but when he denounced the theatre as "the devil's province," St. Denis told him that he was a "narrow old bigot," and quickly left her formal theological studies.

Her rural upbringing was an unlikely home for a "saint" and two stories exist about how she became Ruth St. Denis,[9] and both have charm. After she left her childhood home, St. Denis worked in vaudeville and theatre as both dancer and actress. David Belasco, the famed theatre producer, dubbed her "Saint Dennis" during a run in the production of "Madame DuBarry," "because of her straitlaced personality."[10] At that time, St. Denis was being romanced by noted architect Stanford White, and Belasco was not pleased with her rejection of him. At a party, he talked about her: "No man will ever hold her for long except through her mind. She's all brain."

During her theatrical years, St. Denis was using the stage name of Radha, one of the goddess characters she performed in a dance solo. This name is particularly significant because Radha, historically is often thought of as the god Krishna's primary consort, and their union – Radha-Krishna – signifies the marriage of the feminine with the masculine. According to author Regina Sara Ryan, "The idea as expressed by the Baul sect of India is that the fullness of the Divine principle is 'RadhaKrishna.' The two are inseparable, and their union is the union that each of us must experience internally for the realization of spiritual unification. Whereas Radha was a human woman, she has been deified as a goddess. This is very uncommon in Hinduism, where most goddesses never had a normal human incarnation."[11]

St. Denis's *Radha* solo was one of her most famous. Years later, while Ruth's mother was tagging some luggage for her daughter's dance tour, she changed her stage name from Radha to "St. Denis." "While tagging our innumerable bundles, Mother suddenly looked up, a pencil poised in her hand and said, 'Ruthie, I don't know just what to put on these tags. Up until now we've called you Radha. But as you're going to do other things, I think you ought to use your own name. After all, you are an American dancer, and not an East Indian. What was it that Belasco used to call you? Wasn't it Saint Denis?' 'Yes,' I said, and Mother wrote it on the tag, and thus casually my new name came into being."[12]

Mystical Revelations

During her lifetime, St. Denis experienced many mystical revelations, and these sacred realms provided the firm foundation for her life's work in sacred dance. The written word provided great inspiration for her throughout her life and her love for metaphysical and spiritual writings was acquired well before she was twelve years old, already enjoying *Camille*, The New Testament, and Kant's *Critique of Pure Reason* (even though she confessed that she didn't fully understand the content of the latter). While reading in her parents' study, she picked up a copy of Mary Baker Eddy's *Science and Health with Key to the Scriptures* and this book

Ruth Speaks

When within one personality exists the possibility – and I believe it nearly always does – of the artist and the saint, the efforts of reconciliation dominate one's entire consciousness. I am quite sure that there has never been a saint who has not at some time wished to see limned upon the external world the image of his internal rapture, nor does the artist ever pass a year of his life that he does not wish the whole mechanism of his so-called art life at the bottom of the sea so that he might know true liberation. So if we regard the saint and the artist as two sons of the same mother, we shall perhaps understand them a little better. Many saints have written of the beauty of their own inward states, and to the degree that the words have also been of beauty, so that in the end to some degree the saint does become the artist. But how far the artist becomes the saint is yet to be understood. I do not wish to appear other than I am. Above all not to assume the saint when only the artist is present. – AUL, 47.

permanently changed her. Eddy's words offered her insight into a spiritual world revealing a "a new dimension to my thought and feeling. This definite condition of spiritual ecstasy remained with me for some weeks."

St. Denis's spiritual experience is similar to the spiritual openings that many mystics have had. The ecstasy she described prepared her consciousness to receive input from the universal forces that would shape and guide her life until her death.

Father Andrew Greeley, in his book *Ecstasy: A Way of Knowing*, offers a succinct explanation of the mystic's understanding, which is important in appreciating St. Denis's revelation. "The experience is more one of knowing than of feeling. If anything is heightened in the ecstatic interlude, it is the cognitive faculties of the mystic; [s]he knows something others do not know and that [s]he did not know before. [S]he sees, [s]he understands,[s]he perceives, [s]he comprehends."[13] St. Denis's innate comprehension of the spiritual world led her later on in her life to establish many alternative forms of worship that included the dance: The Society of Spiritual Arts in 1934, the Church of Divine Dance, and the Rhythmic Choir of Dancers.

St. Denis's diaries are laced with her spiritual insights, and she made no apologies for correlating her mystical experience as an artist with the encounters that many saints had with the Divine. During the 1930s, the profession of dancing was considered less than artistic, even scandalous, yet, she was sure that her endeavors could and would elevate dance from merely performance to a religious state.

Although St. Denis would not publicly call herself a saint in the sense of one who is canonized, she would declare herself a prophet when she was eighty-five years old. In a newspaper article, she told an interviewer, "I am now a self-elected prophet. I have been calling myself a prophet for many years – now I mean it."[14] Aside from the fact that St. Denis believed that she earned the right to call herself a prophet, the word has particular meaning in terms of her life's accomplishments. A prophet must see things more clearly than her contemporaries, and not be afraid to give voice to that understanding. "The prophet is a watchman, a servant, a messenger of God, an assayer and tester of the people's ways," St. Denis wrote. "The prophet's eye is directed to the contemporary scene; the society and its conduct are the main theme. Yet his ear is inclined to God. As a witness the prophet is more than a messenger. As a messenger, his task is to deliver the word [of God] as a witness, he must bear testimony that the word is divine…in his words the invisible God becomes audible."[15]

Ruth St. Denis possessed a firm commitment to the integration of both the spiritual and physical components of dance – a commitment that was key to her spiritual philosophies and a guiding principle throughout her life. During the 1920s, there was a plethora of theatricals that focused on religious themes, and medieval pageants became the rage. During a five year span, plays such as "The Tidings Brought to Mary" (1924), "Salut au Monde!" (1921), a collage of religious ceremonies from all over the world, "Kuan Yin," and "The Dybbuk" were popular themes. However, St. Denis's ideas for sacred dances were not the ideas of someone jumping on the commercial bandwagon. She was an excellent businesswoman, but not the type of person who would compromise her art for the sake of financial success as she strived to present an art form that contained spiritual consciousness. Her devotion to the ideals of Mary Baker Eddy and her commitment for the elevation of the arts are themes that do not evaporate or lose their potency over time.

When St. Denis formed the Rhythmic Choir in 1934, her intention was to choreograph dances specifically to be performed in churches with a "new order of religious dancers." This was a radical idea and not everyone in the church audiences appreciated her efforts. In fact, St. Denis initiated the use of dance in modern day churches, and the liturgical dance movement owes her a great debt. Although

Ruth Speaks

My studies in Hindu and Buddhist literature gave rise to Radha, *which I felt at the same time to be a first gesture towards the use of dance as a means of spiritual expression. Such spiritual realization… comes largely although not entirely, from the study of the* Science of Being *as revealed by Mary Baker Eddy. I accept her statement of the real and spiritual identity of humanity, and I wish to found a system of dance on this principle… The exigencies of a public career has often disturbed and suppressed my natural urge towards the atmosphere of spiritual radiation.*

– WCD, 22-23.

she is usually ignored historically in this context, this fusion of dance and religion was one of her proudest accomplishments. Samuel Lewis, the founder of the Dances of Universal Peace, was profoundly influenced by his friendship with St. Denis, and according to Sufi scholar, Kamae A. Miller, Lewis considered her to be the "grandmother" of the dances.[16] He acknowledged her great gifts in his diary when he wrote: "Ruth St. Denis has the faculty of drawing music and dances out of the cosmos, out of the heart-of-God. She has taught me this faculty. Not many people can do that, but with the 'coming race' appearing, more and more are coming into incarnation…On my next trip south, I am to see, God willing, Ruth St. Denis to present to her the 'Dance of Universal Peace.' This has been accepted by world leaders of religion and rejected by cult leaders. As Miss Ruth and I commune, it is not necessary to say much. She wanted to tell me her philosophy, and I said: 'All right, you speak and I'll dance. That made her very happy."[17]

Although, she was profoundly influenced by a wide variety of metaphysical and religious teachings, Ruth claimed that her philosophy was focused on the burning light[18] – referring, of course, to the Divine Spirit, God or Christ. Even so, St. Denis had an enormous cache of friends from all sects of religion, including Judaism. Lazar Saminsky, the musical director for Temple Emanu-El on Fifth Avenue in New York City, was an ardent supporter. She danced in his temple on two occasions.

Her commitment to the divinity of dance in all religions is what separates her from a religious fanatic, for she was a fanatic about God as a reality that the body could contain, and the label of God did not concern her. I wonder if St. Denis ever had the occasion to read the medieval treatise *Solis Splendor*, published in 1542, which said: "The Spirit dissolves the body, and in the dissolution extracts the soul of the body, and changes this body into soul, and the soul is changed into Spirit, and the Spirit is again added to the body, for thus it has stability. Here then, the body becomes spiritual by the strength of the Spirit." This alchemical text[19] describes perfectly St. Denis's view.

She was unafraid to bring the religious dances of other cultures to the stage, although many critics and academics have criticized her for appropriating ethnic dances, and some scholars have told me that she never toured outside of the United States, which is false. St. Denis did extensive research on all of the goddess figures that she presented on the stage. While touring in India she recorded in her diary: "Standing for a moment by the Buddhist ruins near Sarnath, outside of Benares, where Buddha was first preached, I am again aware of hovering forces. I seem to be standing by his quiet side, realizing to some faith degree his sexless, selfless realization of the Infinite. I feel that I touch the very presence of this compassionate and beautiful soul, and I am content." [20]

While she was on tour, St. Denis carried a number of books with her. The mainstay of her reading was consistent and included: *Buddha and the Gospel of Buddhism* by Dr. Ananda Coomaraswami, The Bhagavad Gita, *Little Essays on Love and Virtue* by Havelock Ellis, *Christ and the Indian Road* by Stanley Jones, *The Travel Diary of a Philosopher* by Count Keyserling, *The Gate Beautiful* by Stimpson, *The Gleam* by Sir Francis Younghusband, *God is My Adventure* by Rom Landeau, and the books of Evelyn Underhill.

Underhill's profound impact on her is obvious, as St. Denis often referred to her works. While it would take a lifetime to analyze both women's writing, one quote by Underhill about the artist is especially significant, and may have inspired St. Denis. Underhill wrote: "The greater the artist is, the wider and deeper is the range of this pure sensation; the more sharply he is aware of the torrent of life and loveliness, the rich profusion of possible beauties and shapes…He is always tending, in fact, to pass over from the artistic to the mystical state…The artist is no more or less than a contemplative who has learned to express himself, and who tells his love in colour, speech, or sound: the mystic,

The female body in ascension by artist Ruth Harwood. Courtesy of The Ruth Harwood Papers, Manuscripts Division, Marriott Library, University of Utah.

upon one side of his nature, is an artist of a special and exalted kind, who tries to express something of the revelation he has received, mediates between Reality and the race."[21]

The Mystery of the Goddess

When she was still an actress in the theatre, St. Denis experienced the goddess Isis (who also inspired Duncan), face-to-face, an encounter that compelled her to appear on stage as various deities from diverse cultures. Her list of exalted figures included many representations of the Virgin Mary, as well as Radha (Indian goddess),[22] Kuan Yin (Chinese goddess), Kwannon (Japanese goddess), Pelée (goddess of the volcano),[23] Egypta (the goddess Isis), and Ishtar (Babylonian goddess.). "All of my best works are as goddesses – the cosmic order of life."[24]

Her mystical interlude with Isis did not happen in a "holy place," but in a soda shop in upstate New York as she sipped a soda with a friend. St. Denis and her companion saw a poster of the goddess Isis seated upon a throne. Ruth was so enamored with the poster, she asked her friend to remove it so she could post it on her wall. "This superficial, commercial drawing for a cigarette company opened up to me in that moment the whole story. I identified myself in a flash with the figure of Isis. I knew that my destiny as a dancer had sprung alive in that moment. I would become a rhythmic and impersonal instrument of spiritual revelation. I had never known before such an inward shock of rapture."[25]

An avid reader, St. Denis's interest in Isis led her to research painting, sculpture, and the archeology of Egypt. She wrote: "I have no wish to appear more occult and mysterious than necessary, but I did have a strange intuitive understanding, far beyond anything that I consciously knew, of the great power Egypt wielded over our age and culture. I had glimpsed in the history, religion and art of Egypt, the symbol of man's eternal search for the beauty and grandeur of life. The world of antiquity and the Orient

Ruth St. Denis paid a photographer $5.00 to photograph her as the goddess Isis. Courtesy of The Ruth St. Denis Foundation.

with all its rich poetry of the human soul opened up and possessed me."[26]

Her search did not end with books, however. While she was touring with the play "Madame DuBarry," she found herself in San Francisco with five dollars in her pocket and spent the entire sum to pay a photographer to photograph her costumed as Isis. It was an unusual choice for any woman, but St. Denis was far from a usual woman. About this event she reflected: "In those days, right-minded young ladies did not go about in bare feet, and with only a band of silk around their apparently unclothed middles. Anyone who chooses [to see my picture] will see a serious young person, seated on an improvised throne, which was probably the photographer's one chair, with a dark drape thrown over it. I had on a short black Egyptian wig with a little paper lotus flower in front. Around my ankles and arms is the imitation Egyptian jewelry made out of colored beads. I am seated in the same pose as the poster and looking as stern as a small youthful face can look when obsessed with a grand idea. That poster goes into mysticism."[27]

In 1910, St. Denis created *Egypta*, which premiered at the New Amsterdam Theatre in New York, and it was a major work. Although the score has vanished, and it was never recorded on film, a description of "The Mystery of Isis" (sometimes called "The Veil of Isis") does exist.

Setting: A great temple of columns receding toward the focal point at center upstage, the throne of Isis, shrouded in gloom. There the goddess sits, wrapped in veils edged in heavy gold.

Scenario: Priests glide onstage, bearing votive lights. They make their obeisance to Isis, then quietly withdraw. The voice of a priest is heard offstage, chanting the praises of the goddess. He enters and offers incense, then prostrates at the idol's feet. She stirs. A shaft of light illumines her face and the delicate sweep of her lashes as she slowly comes to life. Isis lifts one hand in benediction. Stepping from her throne, she walks downstage, swaying. She assumes her identity as the goddess of the sky by lifting her veiling to expose the headdress of Hathor, with forked horns cradling a round disk of the moon. Underneath her veils she wears a straight, banded underslip covered with glistening bugle beads. She carries the bow and the arrow of Neith, the great mother-goddess, and indicated with her veils the sweep of the skies, the sunrise, and the sorrow of Isis in her search for her dead consort, Osiris. Then she draws her veils about her and returns to the throne as gloom descends once more.[28]

When she was crisscrossing the country in 1911 on tour, presenting excerpts of her works, including *The Veil of Isis*, the reviews were mixed. Two critics sitting in the same audience during her San Francisco engagement interpreted the program differently, disputing both the talent and esthetic appeal of St. Denis's choreography and dancing. Ralph E. Renaud, a writer for the *San Francisco California Chronicle* found her performance full of "esthetic appeal" and a "fresh point of view."

The other critic in the audience, Frances Jolliffe, did not take to St. Denis' unique talents and presentation, and the review of that evening's performance reads like a personal attack. Jolliffe took no pains to hide the fact that he left the show at intermission missing her now well-known solo, *Radha*.

Negative reviews did not stop St. Denis from continuing to create dances in honor of goddess figures. She wanted to manifest of the Divine Feminine through these deities on the stage. She *became* the goddesses during performances. St. Denis conducted years of research into the Jewish personification of the goddess, Shechinah. She understood that each goddess she portrayed was a part of the One goddess. In choosing various forms of this One she knew she could speak to a broader audience. St. Denis asked her rabbinical friends "What is the meaning of Shechinah?" and delighted in the discussions that followed. "I backed the rabbis into a corner, for my interpretation was really theirs, and my interpretation is that she manifested as a presence of God in a luminous light."[29] Shechinah's roots as "God as Mother,"

The Critics Wrote

"Miss St. Denis has not stopped to learn her art. She shows no training, is unable to keep a pose or a climax. The dancer lacks imagination. Miss St. Denis reveals nothing but heavy ankles. The artist beside me tell me that the Dance of the Five Senses *[also called* Radha *and referred to the five Buddha senses] was worth seeing. Unfortunately, perhaps for me, I did not see it. By that time, my five senses had dropped asleep and it wouldn't have done any good. When the second intermission came I said if I remained any longer it would be my own fault. So I regret not to be able to report upon the last of the program."* – Frances Jolliffe, San Francisco California Bulletin, 4 April 1911. RSD.

evolved from the Canaanite mother goddess Asherah, whom the ancient Hebrews honored until 800 BC when she was removed from the Jerusalem temple, although her worship continued elsewhere.

The definition of Shechinah was appealing to St. Denis. She was the female aspect of God, or "the presence of infinite God in the world, and her presence is intimately connected with the expressions of human love."[30] St. Denis's referred to her as "a luminous light," which is akin to the mystics' descriptions through the centuries of a luminous presence of the Divine. This symbolism was not lost on St. Denis, and she wrote about "Light" as spiritual illumination in a pamphlet that documented her interpretation of Christian symbols.

> As far as we can learn, Light has ever been the symbol for spiritual illumination, naturally its mode or manner of presentation and the shape of its carrier has been different in different ages and cultures. Throughout the scriptures of the world, Light of true learning brings wisdom, and wisdom of spiritual knowledge destroys darkness or ignorance. The Chinese have a wonderfully helpful saying; IT IS BETTER TO LIGHT ONE CANDLE THAN TO CURSE THE DARKNESS. Oh, but how much easier it is to spend time in smoking cigarettes and enjoying oneself, telling somebody who will listen what is wrong with your college, your family, or with your government; than it is to stop and listen and light one small candle of wisdom to illumine the problem which confronts you! Look for the different carriers or receptacles which have brought the light down through the procession of Time. [31]

The Critics Respond

Not since Isadora Duncan had audiences been offered the opportunity to watch sacred dance on stage. When she performed with her company at Carnegie Hall in 1927 (with co-partner Ted Shawn), it was the first time that any non-symphonic artists had ever played to capacity audiences. The performances were sold out. This engagement was an enormous financial success and St. Denis and Shawn "dazzled a nation with the most elaborate costumes, settings and productions that America, very probably, had ever seen."[32]

Yet, Christena L. Schlundt, her biographer, and a dance scholar, writes in a dismissive tone about her accomplishments: "Was there anything in her art that carried meaning to following generations?"[33] Certainly, she was aware of Martha Graham's assessment of St. Denis's work (Graham was St. Denis's student at Denishawn School.) "Miss Ruth was a great and sincere performer. She was always decorative but she was more than that. She had a luminosity, an inward orientation. It's different from power. It's the goddess image."[34] Schlundt shockingly claims that, "Ruth St. Denis left no technique, no theory, no repertory to posterity. Her vaudeville years, her concert years, her trips to the Orient – all add up to a tremendous amount of time but obviously are not important in time. The American dance as a viable, unique art began with the moderns circa 1930 and with Balanchine circa 1935. Anything before that was warmed over European dance,"[35] are not only irresponsible comments, they are without basis. But, the deeper problem with this stance is that it totally ignores St. Denis's spiritual knowledge, wisdom, and contributions.

Jack Anderson, a dance critic, also shared Schlundt's apparent disdain: "I am left with an image of a spirited eccentric who charmed her audiences and kicked up a ruckus. Is this all that can be said of Ruth St. Denis? Or have I missed something?"[36] Clearly, he has. St. Denis's choice of creating choreographic works to the goddess was not a whimsical choice, but a choice based on the recognition of the responsibility and power as an artist that she was able to exercise.

It is only with the restoration of our bodies as instruments of reverence, moral discipline and spiritual realization that we will set to work to evolve a finer life. On the one hand, we have the politicians and the representatives of the divine with the corpulent or underfed bodies covered with the respectable black garments of their several offices, and on the other a well proportioned, beautiful athlete whose only concern is the body. We have women in all professions continuing to progress in heart and brain, but ignoring their bodies, while the ballet dancer's entire concern is with her arabesques and entrechats. It is not that we should specialize less, but that we should humanize more. Our disintegration shows in our bodies as well as in our minds. What single act can polarize and focus the forces of life-physical, emotional and spiritual-like the dance?[37]

Are these the words of a "spirited eccentric"? St. Denis's unique possession of language and of articulation of the mystical experience in her lectures, private papers, autobiography, and poetry make her an important spiritual philosopher, whose contributions should not be ignored.

Delsarte's Influence

Ruth St. Denis was strongly influenced by a performance she watched during the winter of 1892, when her mother took her to watch Genevieve Stebbins, a proponent of the Delsarte system of movement, a popular method during that time. Although many people dismissed the system as nothing more than a series of body movements, it was far more; a fact that is usually ignored. "In its original form, Delsarte's doctrine was a scientific analysis of body gesture and corresponding emotional and spiritual states. His 'Law of Correspondences' assigned a metaphysical equivalent to each physical fact. Delsarte divided bodily movement into three great orders: oppositional movement, with body parts moving in opposite directions simultaneously to express force and power; parallel movements, with body parts moving simultaneously in the same direction denoting physical weakness; and successive movements, which pass through the entire body, expressive of emotion."[38] The "law of correspondences" that he used derived from the Egyptian hermetic philosophy and was already three thousand years old by the time of Christ.

The program that young Ruth witnessed was then termed "statue-posing," and Stebbins performed as the goddess Isis. She became an important influence on St. Denis's lifelong work. Stebbins was the first artist St. Denis saw who was able to integrate the sacred with dance on the stage. "When a child of eleven, I was taken to see Mrs. Stebbins in an unforgettable performance of Greek dancing. My whole artistic life was born at that hour."[39]

"Stebbins's system of movement was what we now consider *modern dance*…[with its] oppositional swings of the arms and legs, foot flexion, spirals, lateral bending of the trunk, subtle shifts of weight, backfalls to the floor. Stebbins built her system of exercises on breath rhythms and emphasized the diaphragm, the great centre muscle, the roof of the stomach and the floor of the lungs. In its rise and fall, contraction and relaxation, it carried with it all muscles attached, and all the vital functions of life are toned and invigorated by its energetic action."[40]

Denishawn

It would be difficult to ignore the similarities between Stebbins' (and perhaps, Delsarte's) work with the dance techniques of both St. Denis and Martha Graham. Although Graham's technique is considered to have originated from herself exclusively, she studied with St. Denis earlier. Graham's dance education, in general, and her signature training style of "breath and release," in particular, probably came from her time at Denishawn, the famous school that St. Denis and husband Ted Shawn founded.

Ruth Speaks

We held steadfastly to the belief that Denishawn should be more than an institution, that it should be a philosophy. We wanted the school to be a stream of ideas. There were classes in music visualization, and in the dance techniques of India, Japan, Egypt, North Africa, Java. We studied plastiques and dramatic gesture, based on Delsarte. Ted [Shawn] gave lectures on the history of the dance and on the philosophy of dance and costumes. I talked on the Orient and about the handling of draperies; other teachers discussed music, color, make-up. Yet, we always taught the fundamentals of barre work.
– AUL, 244.

Denishawn was a revolutionary and unique home for the education of dancers – in mind, body, and spirit. An idyllic environment, for not only the dancer who wanted to learn about dancing, but for the dancer who wanted to learn about life. The forward thinking and visionary ideas of their school were years before their time and, unfortunately, their utopian template has been lost. In most professional dance schools today the emphasis lies in the anatomical understanding of the body coupled with technique and, sometimes, dance history courses. The real education of the spirit, in which St. Denis so fervently believed, is rarely if ever included. She wanted Denishawn to be more than a teaching factory to train dancers in "mere technique," and so these dancers studied the history of cultures, philosophy, and metaphysics.

The *Denishawn Magazine* (which they started) was a remarkable publication that included ideas about choreography, technique, and metaphysical philosophies. The focus of the writing was on the spiritual elements not only of dance, but of all the arts, and the holy implications for such elevated art forms. St. Denis, as well as Shawn, often wrote essays in the magazine. "The real message of Denishawn was the inner ideal to open up to new vistas of life to all those who have the longing to express beauty because Art is the natural intensifying and focusing of this love that is in all human beings to varying degrees. In some it is developed to a remarkable extent, and it is to these [artists] that Denishawn has made its greatest appeal." She was well aware of the powers of her vision for the school and wanted her vision to "go far into the realm of causes and expand into the realms of effect. In a word, we believe that we have touched upon the vital and necessary causes that will in the future lead to a greater and finer manifestation of art than we have ever known."

Based on her extensive metaphysical studies St. Denis used the yin/yang symbol in the magazine to represent the dualities of life. Inside the circle of union, divided by a line, were the images of woman on the left (the receptive side), and man on the right. Her boldly creative manifesto was spelled out beneath the symbol in the magazine.

Denishawn is the creation, in terms of the dance, of the action and reaction of the dualism in the universe. Its expression and philosophy are based on the self-evident spiritual fact that all things are evolved by the action and reaction of the two underlying elements of creation, positive and negative.

Our symbol expresses this dualism unity by two individuals in a unified circle. This symbol includes the images of both man and woman, but the spiritual ideas of these elements is impersonal. In their manifestation they take on these outer forms of man and women but in the actual working out of art creations and in the regenerating and renewing of the individual these elements are understood and used impersonally. In every work of art these are expressed, and in every artist expressing them they exist.

Denishawn, in its outer activities of school and stage, is the visible manifestation of this principle, that life is expressed in harmonious movement, and is so expressed by the constant action and reaction of the basic elements of the divine mind. These elements are impersonal and everywhere expressed in man and in nature, but often in great complexity of character and action, as well is in the so called normal and obvious entities of man and woman.

Dancers of the New Age
We are the dancers of the new
    age!
The revealers of the glory that
    has been shown,
The prophets of the glory that
    is to come.

Within the temple of the dance
We have become priests of the
    new day,
And perform out mighty ritual
    of beauty.

Only obedience to law is liberty,
But that liberty is beauty,
And that law divine.

Hidden from the dull ears and
    veiled from blinded eyes
Is the great rhythm of the
    universe,
And we are the rhythms of the
    law made visible.

We bring you proportion,
    which is order,
Rhythm, which is power,
And, beauty, which is joy.

Behold the vision of your
    greater selves,
The images of your dreams,
Dancing upon the mountains.

O World,
Behold and live again.
We have found the secret,
We have found the way,
It is to dance! – Ruth St.
    Denis, LL, 2-3.

The idea of the completeness of man/woman was a theme St. Denis repeated often, and longed for in her own romantic life. "I am the Soul, the Woman Soul and the Man Soul in one. All capacities are mine, all opposites, all fusions, I am complete!" These ideas were not necessarily revolutionary for the time because the interest in sacred culture and metaphysics garnered unparalleled popularity, but that St. Denis and Shawn would incorporate such high ideals in their dance program had never been accomplished before, or since to my knowledge. It was a magnificent ideal, and her visions and teaching often appeared in her poetry.

St. Denis and her company would successfully tour not only the U.S. – where at the height of her (their) popularity, they had schools on both coasts – but travel to Europe and the Orient until her break-up with Ted Shawn.[41] Many of their students attained fame after they left Denishawn, including silent film star Louise Brooks and dancers/choreographers Martha Graham, Doris Humphrey, and Charles Weidman. Even Louis Horst, the company's beloved musical director, left Denishawn to join his lover, Martha Graham, who was establishing her own company in New York.

Educating the Community

St. Denis truly wanted to convey, in both her art and educational training at Denishawn, the ability to "dance before great audiences to deliver a wordless message of immortality; that life is harmonious without end – because without divinity [one] would not be living, breathing or dancing."[42] The key to St. Denis's contributions to the dance rests with her unceasing commitment to bring the divine component not only onto the stage and into her own body, but to convey that elevated presence to her audience. She, like Duncan, wanted to train children as well as adults to experience the gift of the "Divine dance." In addition to her ideas for a temple of dance, she wanted to create community spiritual sanctuaries for the arts that would be accessible

Ruth St. Denis as the goddess Kwan-Yin.
Courtesy of Jacob's Pillow Photo Archive.

Ruth Speaks

All children should be encouraged to value the divine rhythms which pulsate through their radiant bodies. Every grown person should move with dignity and grace. I do not for one minute advocate swinging to the other extreme by making an idolatry and fetish of the body or of the dance. These are not things to worship in themselves or substitutes for the realization of ourselves as primary spiritual beings. What I do advance is that we should bring our entire being – physical as well as mental – in line with divine will. Then the realization of life in its stupendous vibrations of power and beauty may find a pliable, exquisitely tuned instrument through which to reveal itself instead of the dull, insensitive organism that we too often possess.
– WCD, 83

to young and old. These sanctuaries were not exclusionary – she intended that people from all walks of life would participate. It was a grand idea and echoes the beginnings of the field of "expressive arts therapies," years before this term was even known.

St. Denis's ideas for creating a community outlet for the arts was pioneering, although this community never materialized in her lifetime. She wanted to create "community studios," to be enjoyed by neighborhoods all over the country, as an indication of "the final flowering of its civilized life." But this was not merely an impulse on her part. She was an astute businesswoman and had a plan to achieve her goal. St. Denis intended to ask wealthy patrons to lend a plot of ground for ten years. A committee would be formed, with a hundred or more local families-with-children participating in the program. She planned on asking an architect to donate services and enlist the cooperation of artists, while she would approach businessmen for the financing. She wanted to hire "first-class dancing teachers," at a marketable wage, because she was well aware of the plight of most dance teachers who cannot pay their rent. "One could – and here is the great point of my scheme – give her entire time to teaching and performing instead of worrying about the rent, getting out leaflets to drum up trade, and slowly discovering that the school she loves is turning into a monster which drains her lifeblood without providing for the release of her spirit in which she has dreamed."[43] She wanted these centers to be scattered on the outskirts of all big cities in order to be accessible, and hoped that retired people would participate, believing that through the graphic arts, "Older people would find joy and release in those delayed art expressions which had been denied them. In a word, it was to be a center of free art for the people and by the people."[44]

When she presented her plan during a woman's luncheon in San Francisco, the audience was receptive, but not overly enthusiastic to her ideas. "Perhaps, this was a scheme which belongs to ten or twenty years from now, but I have always cherished it as a solution to a grievous problem." St. Denis's idea was not only novel, it echoed the ideas of other artists of the twentieth century who wanted to create works called *Gesamtkunstwerk*,[45] or total works of art that would embrace the worlds of dance, theatre, painting, and music. However, in St. Denis's case, she wanted to educate ordinary people so they could participate in the healing powers of the arts.

Ruth and Isadora

The similarities between Ruth St. Denis and Isadora Duncan are both notable and provocative, and although they shared celebrity during their respective times, they also shared many spiritual and esthetic ideas. The two women never met in person, although St. Denis did attend two performances of Duncan's. They were often compared, and St. Denis frequently commented on Duncan's work and influence in interviews and magazine publications, as well as in her autobiography.

> I saw Isadora dance in America and in Rome in 1930.[46] I saw Isadora and the Isadorables. The lights focused on the middle of the stage and slipped out and she stood in this light. She lifted her head like a sun worshipper and her hands hung by her side in her Greek costume. The pianist paused and then she paused. It appeared to me that I was a little more sensitive to the process of dancing. She invoked the spirit of the dance and she put herself under the spirit of the Divine. She offered herself. She began to sway and the true rhythm was from inside. She lifted from her solar plexus and turned her head and it was beautiful. She was an exalted human being while she was dancing. She exalted the simplicities of the soul of the human being. Every consciously divine dancer has a coordination of the inner nerves of rhythm and the energies – all of the unseen ones as

they flowed outward was the spectacle of her dance. She represented "the dance" more than I did.[47]

Duncan's approach to technique was vastly different than St. Denis's, because St. Denis utilized the ballet barre basics in her training, and Duncan deplored the rudiments of ballet. However, each of them shared a spiritual philosophy about the dance's divine purpose as well as the belief that through the observance of dance, the audience members would be able to experience a type of elevated consciousness. The similarities of their ideas are striking. Ironically, both artists performed in theatricals and vaudeville programs as "ballet dancers," even though they loathed the form. According to St. Denis, "When I was 10 or 12 years old, I attended ballet class and Madame Bonfanti, the ballet teacher, threw me out. I was falling all over myself."[48] And in Isadora's case, "The ballet school taught pupils that the spring of movement was found in the center of the back at the base of the spine. From this axis, they said, arms, legs, and trunk must move freely, giving the result of an artificial puppet. This method [of training] produced an artificial mechanical movement not worthy of soul.[49] Since my mother was very poor our neighbors knowing of my dancing ability urged my mother to let me dance so I could earn money. And so, out of necessity, when I was four years old, I was forced to dance before the public. That is why I don't like children to dance before the public for money, because I have experienced what it means to dance for a piece of bread."[50]

François Delsarte, the French scientist of movement and anatomy, influenced both women mostly in terms of technique, although they didn't study with him directly. When they were children, literally thousands of people were teaching the Delsarte system of movement. "In March 1898, *The Director* published an interview in which Isadora stated that Delsarte, 'The master of all principles of flexibility, and lightness of body should receive universal thanks for the bonds he has removed from our constrained members.'"[51]

Ruth's mother, a most unusual woman, was responsible for teaching her daughter the Delsarte doctrine. Ironically, Mrs. Denis taught her the Delsarte system of movement, believing that it would *tame* her child's spirit. St. Denis would later utilize this methodology at Denishawn.

St. Denis's ideas for what she termed "the divine dance" were concepts that she articulated not only in her lectures to her students at Denishawn, but in lectures on dance throughout the country. Her journals are filled with poetry and essays (similar to Duncan's vision for the "Dance of the Future") that articulate the necessity to bring the spiritual components into the training of the dancer. Like Duncan, who said that she was taught to dance by the muse Terpischore, St. Denis claimed, "The movement I have the Lord taught me."[52] Both were self-proclaimed prophets of dance and their ideas were years before their time.

St. Denis was a metaphysician and a voracious reader like Duncan, and was also well acquainted with the significance of color, so much so, that she wrote a treatise on the subject entitled "The Color Dancer." Mistakenly, many academics have attributed her understanding of color to the influence of Delsarte's books. Perhaps the initial reading of one text, which included a chapter on color, did remain in her thoughts. However, it is much more likely that she obtained her color education from theosophical readings and books about color that were published during that time. "The Color Dancer" appeared in *Denishawn Magazine* and suggested compelling ideas replete with imaginative and rich images for color and lighting on stage.

Like Duncan, St. Denis was also fascinated with the effects of color upon the body and worked with Thomas Wilfred, an inventor and singer who created the Clavilux organ, a device that emitted polymorphous fluid streams of light in response to music. He called it "Lumia" and its inspiration stemmed from his desire, along with his fellow members of the theosophy movement, to demonstrate the spiritual principles of color using a self-contained mechanical

"A Color Dancer is one whose color sense is predominant over her musical sense, whose being responds instinctively and intelligently to color in all that she expresses. As a creative artist, she deals primarily with color and form, and as an interpretive artist she instinctively chooses those themes of emotions that are related to color, rather than to pure tone or pure rhythm. We have too long regarded color as a superficial or subsidiary element, at least in the art of the stage; whereas the vibration which results in color is no less fundamental than the vibration that results in tone. Color is an intelligent art, and the sister art to dance." – Ruth St. Denis, Denishawn Magazine, *Vol. 1(2) 1-4.*

It [the sari] is not really a dress, but a strip of clothing draping the body. It provides not only a skirt and waist but with a few twists and turns, a scarf for the head as well. I think when the sari is adapted for Western use, we will make an important step in common sense dressing. At the beginning of my career, I decided that ordinary women's clothing hampered my movements of both the professional dancer and for women in general. I told my students to wear a one piece bathing suit in the studio to practice. – IRSD

unit. Wilfred was a friend of architect Claude Bragdon, one of St. Denis's closest friends, and no doubt Bragdon orchestrated the meeting between them at the Ramakrishna-Vivekananda Center in New York, where the three often attended meetings. Historically, their introduction was quite important, but is little more than a footnote in texts.

Wilfred believed that "Light was the artist's sole medium of expression. He must mold it by optical means, almost as a sculptor models clay. He must add color, and finally motion, to his creation. Motion, the time dimension, demands that he must be a choreographer in space."[53] In an article in *Denishawn Magazine*, St. Denis spoke about her experimental work with Wilfred. "While in New Hampshire one summer, I made the first experiment, I believe, that has been made with the art of mobile color and body movement. Mr. Wilfred was most interested in making this experiment with me in relation to his color organ, and we both felt that new and beautiful returns will eventually come out of this alliance." She never mentioned their association in terms of her spiritual development, or the continuation of their alliance. However, the topics of light and color are two themes that she returned to again and again in her published and unpublished writings.

Both women never wore shoes, and Duncan wore a tunic as her daily dress because this loose flowing costume offered her ultimate freedom of the body and liberation from social and physical confines. St. Denis preferred to wear a sari. The fact that St. Denis chose to wear a sari was a demonstration of her freedom of dress because it was practical, unconventional, and beautiful. She understood, like Duncan, that freedom of dress was a metaphor for liberation of thought.

A master of costumes, her friend Walter Terry was so interested in her work that he conducted a laboratory session in the late 1950s to examine her techniques, investigating how her "use of weight, color, and texture of the materials she chose were aligned to her gestural patterns."[54]

Unfortunately, he never specified how he conducted these sessions, but wrote in *Miss Ruth*: "Her concept on the use of draperies and properties was firmly based in a belief that for the dancer, draperies represented an extension of the movements of the body into the space. No one, not even Loie Fuller [who was known for her craft at using draperies before Isadora Duncan], exploited materials with such esthetic perceptivity."[55] Like Duncan, St. Denis recognized the freedom given to the body, a woman's body, when the corset and other tight pieces of clothing were eliminated.

Both women were not interested in merely posturing in their dances and sought to elevate their choreography and distinguish it from merely decorative dance. Steadfastly devoted to their discipline as dancers, each of them danced until the end of their lives[56] and, until her death, St. Denis continued to both exercise and meditate each day, using a carpet she called her "gimmick." At age eighty-four, she provided a visual explanation to Walter Terry, her close friend and journalist who was writing an article about her. At that time, St. Denis was working on an illustrated book she called *Vita Nuova, The New Life.* In it she described "essential breathing exercises and stretches and suggestions for musical background." When she was finished demonstrating the exercises, she rolled up into a headstand.

> No one can expect the average woman to exercise to the degree that we dancers do, but if they want a new life, and they want to live longer they can't let the body rust. It has to be used. And my package plan is designed to keep it from rusting.[57]

The discipline of the dancer and the discipline of the mystic who spends countless hours in prayer are apt since both arts demand absolute practice and commitment and both St. Denis and Duncan lived that discipline and commitment.

St. Denis maintains that, during the first twenty years of her performing career, she was not at all cognizant of "having any intellectual credo."[58] However, her pull to the spiritual is apparent in her poem "I Have A Line, A Destiny," written in 1919 when she was forty-one. Upon reflection, it is obvious that St. Denis already understood the spiritual path that she had traveled, at the midpoint of her lifetime.

The Temple

Throughout her life, St. Denis wanted to create a temple where the arts would be dedicated as instruments of worship. She had a vision for this temple when she and her dance group returned from a tour of the Orient. Although her dancers possessed various religious and spiritual beliefs, St. Denis felt that "there was one common need which drew us together, the need of touching the eternal Realities of Existence."[59] Out of her vision was born the Society of Spiritual Arts (Church) based in Hollywood, California in 1934, although the underpinnings of this group began during her days at Denishawn.

> I was lying out on the couch that was always placed in my dressing room and with hands clasped behind my head, in that half-wakeful, half-sleeping state which is so often the perfect condition for creative thought. For some moments, feeling the silence of the theater, I remained in a state of quivering expectancy. Suddenly, looming like a great pearl — like a new Taj Mahal — against the dark shadows of my mind, was a temple. I realized at once that this temple was the symbol and focusing point of my whole dancing life.[60]

St. Denis wanted her temple to be accessible to "the artist, the mystic, the lover, the acolyte, and all those who are filled with the Divine urge to express Beauty through worship...We have no place, no sanctuary where Artists dedicated to God can work in unity. It is to fulfill this urgent need that I long to see this Temple manifested."[61] This synthesis of arts and religion that she envisioned could be duplicated all over the country, and she wanted "replicas of the temple in simpler forms spreading…beginning with the simple cell of a community temple – a single studio – for a mere handful of students and celebrants, and gradually unfolding, as is the organic law of life, into more complex forms. I saw many churches opening their doors hospitably to this hitherto unrelated art, the dance. My concept of these new forms of worship, which would include rhythmic movements in our church services, demanded a new and vital expression that would bring humanity into a closer and more harmonious relationship with the One who created our bodies as well as our souls. I also believed that great motion pictures would carry a radiant manifestation of these rituals, so that they would be spread all over the world."[62] It was an enormous vision.

Before the Hollywood establishment of the Society, the organization presented its dances and lectures in various churches in New York City during the mid 1930s, where she received an enthusiastic reception from clergy members including Dr. Fosdick at Riverside Church, Dr. Shoemaker at the Episcopal Calvary Church, and Dr. Wylie at the Presbyterian Church.[63] The latter appearance was covered by the Associated Press in a story amusingly captioned: RUTH ST. DENIS DANCES *HYMN* IN NY CHURCH, TINTED TOENAILS FLASH IN PSALM INTERPRETATION BEFORE ALTAR. The reviewer wrote: "A symphony of white, black and red, the dancer went through motions which she said symbolized 'the gradual descent of man's soul from the moment he acknowledges his need of spiritual light to the final radiation.'"[64] Her appearance attracted a large crowd and even Reverend Wylie said that he had "never realized the greatness of her interpretation of spiritual themes until I saw her myself." She made sure that she presented her spiritual programs in

I have a line, a destiny, a plan
    which I must follow.
My soul beheld itself in
    majesty
In Egypt, in India, in Syria,
    in China.
Always in majesty…in
    power…in stillness.
This was the form, the design
That was given me at the
    beginning.
It is now and ever will be with
    me.
My life runs like a thread
    through the beads of time,
The image does not change.
It is ever white,
It is ever royal,
It is ever still.
I have a line, a destiny, a plan
    which I must follow.
– IRST. Ruth St. Denis,
Poems of Destiny.

various sects of Christian churches as her intimacy with the Divine continued.

St. Denis intuitively knew that her concept of dance as sacred would not only be inspiring for dancers to perform inside a church, but that it could also educate the church members about the sanctity and beauty of the dance. Most importantly, it would provide a worship service *through* the dance, not just pretty entertainment. Her ideas were not limited to the dance, for she envisioned a place where "the expression of all phases of the arts, music, dancing, architecture, sculpture, painting, writing would take place and in the end it will be for the Glory of God."[65] Unhappy with the current thinking towards the arts as commercial and void of any spiritual content, St. Denis was quite articulate about her feelings regarding the attitudes in society, as well as the attitudes of artists who "dance and paint from the surface instead of from the depths. So much of our art that is born of this discordant chaotic age becomes the mighty seducer, the false god which we ignorantly worship instead of holding aloft the vision of Perfection without which the people perish."[66]

Along with the establishment of the Society of Spiritual Arts, St. Denis wrote a manifesto of sorts for the Society, explaining its goals and purposes, and these ideas were published in small leaflets that the Society would create, in her autobiography, her poetry, and her lectures. Some of the subjects for her lectures included: "How Can the Arts Serve Civilization?"; "The Influence of the Arts on the Unfoldment of the Three-Fold Man"; "Unity of All the Arts in One Great Ideal: The Temple"; and "Rhythms of Resurrections: How Many Can Resurrect His Own Life."

The art form of dance, St. Denis believed was and had received a low status – one that was devaluing and disrespectful – and she often spoke of her displeasure. "Dance is degraded to the narrow limits and low level of professionalism – of mere mechanical proficiency, always associated with the most frivolous and ephemeral phases of the stage.

But, this day is fading. We are slowly advancing beyond this stage of obscuration and perversion. We are seeking our gaze inward, learning to seek there the divine sources of the dance. In, we have used almost exclusively the language of the intellect – speech – to express all stages of our consciousness, and by doing so we have inhibited and dwarfed the physical and emotion beauty of the self, while the spiritual consciousness has sought entirely other means of expression, not knowing that dancing in its nobler uses is the very temple and word of the living spirit."[67]

Oddly, her founding and creation of the Society of Spiritual Arts is mostly undocumented in most dance history books or in books written about her life, yet for St. Denis it was her greatest achievement. Although she was brought up in a Protestant home and her mother was no stranger to religious and spiritual writings, St. Denis considered herself, at the end of her life, "a metaphysician."[68] She always considered the art of dance as a calling similar to a call to prayer that a mystic experiences.[69] In an interview she explained: "I suppose that the dance comes under the head of priesthood. Ask a chap in a seminary who becomes a priest, well, he has duties and his real function is to bring the doctrines and fundamentals of the religion to the congregation. The dance will eventually bring him back to himself. In my study of metaphysics, the aesthetics of life, and as a student of the best branches of metaphysics, I know that dance has always been religious and that the body moved with the religion of song. David danced for God, it goes back to the Old Testament. I was the first dancer to dance in a Christian altar, that was my contribution."[70]

When she decided to create her vision of a "dancing church," she continued to write poetry, to lecture, and to make contacts in various houses of worship. At this time in the late 1920s, she was still considered America's leading dancer, and it must have been quite a shock to many of her fans to listen to her speak and dance in a church. According to close friend and dance critic Walter Terry, not everyone

"God speaks to me in the morning. And I write what He has spoken. And I sing what He has told me. God speaks to me in the Golden Noon, and I live on the sustaining and revolving earth, and I am warmed by the rays of His great sun. God speaks to me in the night, And the essence of all beauty and love Has timeless, spaceless being in my soul." – Ruth St. Denis, LL, 12.

When Ruth St. Denis was developing her ideas for her temple, she spoke about producing "religious art in its highest sense; for the instrumentation of tone and color, of form and rhythm . . . employed to release the spiritual consciousness of man into terms of beauty, and would not limit it to any one sect of any one religion. God should be honored, I believed not with old and decaying forms but with the full compliment of those arts and scientists which are daily being unfolded by artists."– AUL, 338.

was pleased about her efforts, and she received some hate mail. One churchgoer considered her performance a "distinct attack against the purity of the Church," to which St. Denis replied in print: "We do not abandon human speech, although songs are sung and speeches made that are obscene. In a word the human voice is neither moral or immoral. It is a neutral instrument of expression and I claim the same thing for the rhythm of the human body."[71] In her defense, Terry wrote several articles on religious dance and was unafraid to come to his friend's side publicly in print. "I hope that one day every American will be able to dance his faith, whatever it may be. At the expense of being branded a mystic, (which is inconceivable in a Connecticut Yankee), I would like to say that those who participate in the rhythm, the pattern of movement and the beauty of the dance must certainly feel themselves as part of the unseen power…This religious dance is not the superficial symbol of an archaic creed; it is the outward manifestation of man's faith…I want to pay tribute to Ruth St. Denis the world's greatest living dancer and one of America's truly great women.[72]"

St. Denis was committed to her quest to build her temple in Southern California. Jack Cole, a former student and a well-known choreographer of stage and film, told Walter Terry, "She wants a *temple!* Why the hell anyone wants a temple in California…She's earned the right. She can have her temple and do anything she wants with it – have Buddhist rituals or pee on the floor. I'll pay for it because she's a genius."[73]

St. Denis wrote a poem entitled "Temple Vision," and although it was never published, it illustrates her command not only of language, but of her understanding of the mystical dimensions of the dance.

Temple Vision

Turning! Turning!
In the Divine Dance of ecstasy.

Our arms are the thousand-petaled lotus
    of your perfect law.

Unfolding, uncurling, weaving, waving
In the golden hours of nirvanic bliss.
Dancing, dancing in the ceaseless rhythms of the stars.
Whirling in the azure spaces of the soul

Moving to unheard voices of the suns.
Turning, turning,
Swinging, swinging,
Dancing, dancing,
Endlessly!

The Divine Dance of Creation forever unfolding in
the sacred bodies of Man and Woman! Patterns of
Divine geometry drawn by living Dancers on the
floor of the temple courts and made plain on the
altar screen for all to see.[74]

St. Denis's vision for a "Temple standing in the
sun…Alive, alight, aglow with the radiated rhythms of the
soul,"[75] is poetry that stands up alongside some of the greatest mystical poetry of any time. Her uncanny ability to
express the world of ecstasy and mystical experience reveals
her as a woman in full command of her talents, able to convey her philosophies with power in her poetic works. The
poem describes the ancient sacred ritual of *sema*, practiced
by the Sufis who utilized sacred turning as a form for their
divine prayers. "*Sema* comes from the words 'to hear,' 'to listen.' It is a listening with the heart in which all thoughts are
dropped from the mind and the devotee listens to the music
with their whole being with the intention of opening to the
eternal presence of God."[76]

"In the earliest days of the development of *sema*, a few
devotees would gather together. Perhaps one would play a
ney or a drum, and someone with a beautiful voice would

begin to sing. The others would sit in silence listening, the beauty and sacredness of the music drawing them closer and closer to God. When one of those sitting felt the music fill and lift them, they would get up and move, letting the sound transport them until they were no more, only the music and the moving remained."[77] Reading St. Denis's words of "turning, unfolding, uncurling, whirling" suggest that she was quite familiar with this ancient ritual, and her words parallel the following eloquent verse by Rumi:

> Dancing is not rising to your feet painlessly like a speck of dust blown around in the wind. Dancing is when you rise above both worlds, tearing your heart to pieces and giving up your soul.[78]

In her autobiography, St. Denis mentions her meeting with an East Indian man named Mehta, who was a "prophet after my own heart."

> We saw a tall, slender East Indian, with a strong and supple body, and a remarkable head. He looked like a young eagle with marvelous far-seeing eyes, a curious beaked nose, which on a lesser personality would have thrown the whole composition of his face out of beauty, but which with him not only fitted his keen mind but added great distinction to his aristocratic bearing.

> After a pleasant talk he put back a rug and began to speak, and presently to move. It seemed to me that for the first time since the days of Mrs. Stebbins, I had found someone who moved as I believe I move. I can express it in this way because it is so obvious that neither Mr. Mehta nor I created that quality of movement which I am speaking of, any more than he created his brown eyes, or I my blue…making his body an instrument for the unending currents of life

to flow through, I kept saying to myself, "Yes, yes, that is what I feel." Before my eyes his movements seem gradually to relate themselves to the natural forces of movement.[79]

Choreography of the Virgin

Over her lifetime, St. Denis performed hundreds of programs in which she danced in honor of the Virgin Mary, but she frequently used various names including: *The Blue Madonna*[80] *[of St. Mark's], Masque of Mary, The Gold Madonna,* and *Queen of Heaven.* According to her longtime confidante and the former director of the Ruth St. Denis Foundation, Karoun Tootikian, "When Ruthie did the *Gold Madonna* and the *Blue Madonna,* she just changed the color of the crown, but the dance was the same, she liked to do that for the Madonna dances."[81] St. Denis's metaphysical inclinations beautifully merged with the dances to the Virgin Mary that she created, recognizing Mary as a goddess, and a source of inspiration for her.

When she created her first dance to the Virgin Mary, it was an idea to which she had given great thought. She wrote: "In the future, I hope to produce Mary, the Madonna. Mary was to symbolize the ultimate creating principle which embraces compassion as well as creation. Mary is the conceiving principle which contains no element of error, discord, or *the limitations of time and space.* This treatment of our Christian goddess was to be done in a modern and not a traditional manner, having many elements which had not been developed in Catholic symbology. My *Mary* is still to be done in her totality. She has appeared today only in fragments."[82]

St. Denis not only wanted to *become* Mary, as she had become her other goddesses on stage, but sought to integrate the spiritual aspects of Mary, the mother, within a woman's body – hers. This was the only way that she could reconcile the centuries long religious split between the intellect (spirit) and the body, which was considered lesser. To

"My Whole body has filled with light. I pour forth my spirit into Joy!
I sing! I dance! I am arrayed in white, for my suffering and fears have
departed from me." – Ruth St. Denis, LL, 4.

117

One of the most beautiful portraits of the Madonna as portrayed by Ruth St. Denis.
Courtesy of Jacob's Pillow Photo Archive.

choose the Mother of Christ, a woman who was pure, a virgin, and free from all human sin, as the subject in her choreography, was the ultimate demonstration, simply because her Mary was *full of self, of body, of woman.* In the Gnostic texts from the second century, knowledge of the divine aspects of the body is pivotal to awakening to a higher consciousness. "These texts suggest that awakening and salvation will come from gnosis; knowledge, including knowledge of the body: If one does not understand how the body which [s]he wears came into existence, [s]he will perish with it...and to someone who will not know the root of all things, they remain hidden."[83]

St. Denis accurately understood that the tools to her spirituality were *through* her body. Although she was "set apart from time and space" and "unrelated to human things in the ordinary sense," she believed that her "body was the willing recipient of the mind and that its geometric forms [dance movements] are the very patterns and designs of divinity."[84] For a dancer to bring mind and body to the dance is, in itself, not the courageous idea, although it is more easily said than done. But the idea that her body could portray the energies of the Divine Mother in the dance and be used by Divine forces is, and was, a revolutionary and elevated concept. Here lies the genius of St. Denis's contributions to the dance.

In her poem "Eternal Mary," quoted in the Introduction (see p. xxiv), she keenly illustrates the belief that we are all capable of possessing love, for ourselves, for our fellow human beings, and for all living things. The idea that "we are all Mary" signifies the possibility that we, too, can become divine human beings by allowing ourselves "to bear the Christ child," and to carry this love within us. Is not her message, the message of Christ consciousness or love consciousness, the same message that is available to all of us, regardless of our religious orientation? Most religions emphasize that the way to God (no matter which God one may choose) is the way of love.

St. Denis spoke of her vision for offering this experience – the "way of love" – to her audience members when she told a reporter, "Our dance has not done anything yet. We might serve the audience, but we have to develop a gesture that would be capable of making every person in the audience say, I am Brahma."[85] This statement is significant because St. Denis was considered a prominent dance artist, and whether she performed in a stadium or a church, she brought to her audiences not only a performance but a divine prayer through dance, that *was* worship, not entertainment.

I have not seen any of St. Denis's dances in honor of the Virgin Mary directly because they do not exist on film (to my knowledge), but I did watch a lovely recreation of *The Gold Madonna,*[86] originally presented by The Denishawn Repertory Dancers, on September 29, 1991, in New York City. This solo is a dramatic, powerful piece. Although the movement is not on a grand scale, it embraces the viewer. The piece opens with the Madonna seated on a chair pointing her finger above her, toward God. She moves slowly off the chair and stretches her arms as if to embrace an invisible presence. As she moves, she picks up a flower and dances with it and descends to a prayer position. After a long pause, quiet and reposed, she arches her back and this exaggerated movement seems to contain all of a mother's suffering. The piece ends as she outstretches her arms again and slowly returns to her prayerful pose.

In an interview, St. Denis said that the inspiration for the *Gold Madonna* (also called *The Masque of Mary*), came to her when she was in Venice visiting St. Mark's Cathedral, and she noticed an image of the Madonna on the ceiling. She hired a composer to rewrite music by the fourteenth century composer Gabrielli. Although she never identifies a recording that she had heard, St. Denis calls it "a devil of a recording."[87]

It is virtually impossible to chronicle all of St. Denis's dances to the Virgin Mary because she often repeated the choreography and substituted names for the dances. Sometimes she would integrate portions of a shorter Madonna piece into a much larger one. *Color Studies of the Madonna*, for example, was the same dance as her first Madonna work, *Masque of Mary*. This dance began with the organ prelude "Dance of Praise," and was followed "by a reading from the Gospels concerning the Immaculate Conception."[88] She was clothed in white veils (symbolizing purity), and stood on an altar, while around her danced the angels. At the end of this dance, as the Madonna she, "removed her veils to reveal her deep turquoise gown."[89] It was an appropriate choice because blue is often the Virgin's color and St. Denis believed it was the color of truth. In various pageants she changed her veils; the red of Nativity (a color associated with the emotions), purple for the Crucifixion (purple has always been a color assigned to priests and other high members of the clergy symbolizing the Divine), and the gold of the Assumption (gold symbolizes divinity).[90]

In California at the Holyrood Episcopal Church in 1934, where St. Denis was scheduled to present *Masque of Mary*, the church rector tried to convince his parishioners to support the program by reminding them of the biblical verse, "Let them praise His name in the dance."[91] At that time (and in some cases in our time), however, the idea for the divine dance in churches was too controversial, and the concert was never presented there. The program was finally done at the Rutgers Presbyterian Church in New York, and it was so successful that it was repeated, and more than seventeen hundred churchgoers were witness to St. Denis's vision. When she presented *Masque of Mary* at Calvary Church in New York, her friend and advocate, Reverend Sam Showmaker, wrote in the program: "I have known and admired Ruth St. Denis for many years, as a great human being and a great interpreter of spiritual truth through art, especially her supreme art of the dance. It was my privilege to baptize her...She has done pageants and dances in my

Ruth Speaks

When I gave a ritual of Masque of Mary, *with the rhythmic choir, at Riverside Church in New York, here, perhaps the first time in a Christian temple, was my initial gesture toward the production of a Christian Temple dance. I had the consciousness that the audience understood the symbolism of the pageant, in the same way as an audience attending a Noh drama understands the symbolism of its Buddhistic faith. – AUL, 365.*

church, always with great reverence as well as great beauty of performance."[92]

Even the critics took notice, including a mention in the *New York Times,* which also added information about "weekly dance rituals on Thursday evenings"[93] held at her Society of Spiritual Arts. She presented the same repertoire during the next few years in New York City, including programs at the Riverside Church, Rutgers Presbyterian Church, Calvary Church, MacDowell Club, the Plymouth Church of the Pilgrims in Brooklyn, and even at the American Common at the World's Fair in New York in 1939, and in Pittsburgh at the Carnegie Music Hall.

When St. Denis presented *Color Study of the Madonna* (which many dance scholars believe was the *Masque of Mary,* and most likely was) at Carnegie Chamber Music Hall in New York, she included a lecture on the role of spirituality and the arts, concluding the program with *Color Study of the Madonna.* One reviewer described the performance as bringing "matchless beauty of gesture and through the warmth of her portrayal, the unending compassion of the Virgin for mankind was revealed."[94] Another critic from a smaller paper wrote, "After the second part had gotten off to a pretentious start with two religious portraits, Miss St. Denis's 'Color Study of the Madonna' and Mr. Shawn's study of 'St. Francis of Assisi,' the first of which, particularly, failed to ring true because of its attitudinizing – the program suddenly came to life casting off their cosmic ways."[95]

Ruth would make fun of her "attitudinizing" and of herself as a self-proclaimed "prophet of dance," although it is clear that she believed that she was a prophet, at least a minor one. "I'm afraid that I shall never be a major prophet because, alas, major-prophets have no sense of humor. Only minor prophets can see how funny it is to have one's head in the Church and one's feet on the stage!"[96]

Her final work in honor of the Madonna was called *The Blue Madonna.* This performance was quite special since she was going to dance at Jacob's Pillow, the legendary dance theatre and studio that her partner, and still-husband, Ted Shawn had founded. Although, the pair never divorced, and each went their own romantic way, they chose not to divorce. The performance of St. Denis and her pairing with Shawn in July 1959 was electrifying, and earned them both rave reviews. It didn't matter that she was in her eighties, she still possessed the magic that had made her a star throughout her life. She also knew about the art of draping the body, and make-up secrets that contributed to her gorgeous form.

"The Blue Madonna of St. Mark's" set to ecclesiastical music, the legendary star gave us three aspects of the Madonna: the Mother with the Child, the Mother at the cross, Mary leading a dance of praise for the glory of Heaven. Beautiful of presence, Miss St. Denis conveyed the three moods of her work through gestures of poetic piety.[97]
– Walter Terry, July 1, 1959

Wayne Smith, a local critic, described her performance that evening when she was "gowned in a large enveloping robe of rich blue colors and gold borders."[98] Impressed, he described her dancing as, "… spiritually uplifting and dramatically exciting work, danced by Miss St. Denis with a greater artistry and force than we have seen performed by her for many years. She still remains a great living force in the theater of dance"[99] She was eighty-one years old.

The Mother/The Mystic

Because Ruth St. Denis walked a spiritual path throughout her life and, perhaps, as she believed, danced "because of God," she no doubt identified with the image of the Virgin Mary as supreme goddess of all cultures.

St. Denis never had children and yet often called herself "mother." However, she understood that her role as prophetess of dance was to bring the majesty of the divine body through the woman, as she tried to do in her dances

At age fifty-one, St. Denis danced one of her many Madonna incarnations, and critic Harro Melle wrote:

"Ruth St. Denis brings before the public a face which in artistic value rates highly as an artist performance in itself and mirrors intelligence . . . The puff of thin white hair is like the finishing touch to a sensitive painter's creation. She is a wonderful subject for poets, and I can very well imagine that even hard-boiled gentleman of the press had lyrical notions describing her . . . One might call her "the embodied glow of a spirit." She knows how to handle silky scarves with heavy embroidery in a masterly way, draping herself in them as though she has never worn anything else. Her "Madonna" is a gothic impression, partly on account of the structure of her body and partly because of her ability to represent Purity and majesty. It is as if El Greco himself has draped her to pose for one of his saints." – Harro Melle, BWTF, 320.

Ruth St. Denis as the Madonna taken at Riverside Church in New York.
Courtesy of Jacob's Pillow Photo Archive.

to the Virgin Mary. Like the little known mystic of the seventeenth century, Joanna Southcott, St. Denis believed, "This is a New Thing Amongst mankind, for a woman to be the Greatest Prophet that ever came into the World, to bring man out of darkness, into My marvelous light."[100]

It is true that our Christian theological concepts have attempted to bring in the feminine principle through the image of the Virgin. But has not the emphasis on her purity influenced us to believe that the act of life between a man and a woman is carnal in itself, whereas it seems obvious to me that it is the attitude of the mind governing that act which degrades it or lifts it up. The word "purity" has been used in a mistaken or negative sense, instead of its true meaning of "unadulterated." Let us remember that the period of gestation, the act of birth, the fondling and loving of a baby by the mother are no less and no more physical than the act of intercourse between a man and a woman. In a word, this virginal conception of the feminine principle has laid a ban on the act of intercourse, a disapproval, and a pronouncement of evil which in my mind has done incalculable harm to the children so conceived and brought into the world.[101]

St. Denis not only recognized the Light that Southcott had spoken of, but she was privy to its encounter. When a friend sent her "a certain volume," she read the chapter on "Christ and Sex," because she was battling her own demons about sex at that time. Still married to Shawn, although they hadn't lived together in decades, St. Denis had a lover who was younger than she, which prompted a great deal of guilt. Coupled with the making of her first dance to the Virgin Mary, she had reached what she described as, "the limit of sin and wretchedness." This book spoke to her and when she read the words, "Ask Christ," she did, and he appeared

The Great Circle

In childhood
I roamed the hills
In search of the great Joy
For I knew I was born know-
ing that it existed.
I saw before me the sacred
fires.
Through which, if I were
To dance and prophesy,
I must pass
As an initiate of the Flame.
Behold I saw a cross
And laid myself on it.
I knew the last final yielding
Of my lesser selves,
My own Truth had destroyed
them.
I was laid waste as a desert
ruin
Where once a city of false
beauty stood.
When this was finished
I beheld a Great Circle
That was concealed behind the
cross.
I saw it become visible with
celestial light.
My body, that hung dead and
bloodless
Upon the cross,
Shone with new radiance.
– Ruth St. Denis, LL,63.

to her in a vision. "The living presence of Christ filled all space and yet seemed as intimate as a friend. In the depths of my own dark and lonely soul I had seen the divine Image, and heard the Immortal Word. I had unconsciously attempted to feed my mystic nature with the food of the intellect and cultivate my spiritual centers by the techniques of metaphysics and all the time my soul was hungry for that strange instantaneous union with Christ which produced peace and fruitfulness. The three preoccupations of my soul – art, religion and love – lay clear and bare before me. Now beauty was the face of God."[102]

When St. Denis refers to "the Immortal Word," it is symbolic of the mystical encounter according to St. John: "In the beginning was the Word, and the Word was with God, and the Word was God."[103] St. Denis not only experienced a mystical union with God, but through the embodiment of Mary, a feminine face of God, she was able to relive and offer to her audiences, in various settings, the love that she experienced during that moment with God. That unending and unconditional love was not only the love she felt with the Christ presence, but the love that Mary felt for her son. The message of love is clear throughout St. Denis's writings and her choreography. Her union with God, the mystical union, was authentic.

As noted previously, St. Teresa wrote: "God establishes himself in the interior of this soul in such a way, that when she returns to herself, it is wholly impossible for her to doubt that she has been in God, and God in her."[104] St. Denis had apparently found herself established in the interior of God.

Ruth St. Denis believed that "every good performance partakes of the elements of love and one's whole performance moves to a climax of joy…the artist feels that he was won the beloved…when in its final brief moment of beauty gives meaning and purpose to the long continuity…touches the eternal Reality."[105] That Reality was her offering to both God and to the people who saw her dance. In my opinion, Ruth St. Denis was a mystic of the highest order. Although her works may not endure, her philosophies and theories about what I term "dance theology" shall.

When St. Denis died, Martha Graham, her former student and another pioneer of modern dance wrote a tribute:

> It is difficult to speak about anyone so essentially living and eternal as Ruth St. Denis, who is now considered to be dead…Her attitude to dance as an almost religious medium and the influence of her magic as a force in dance on all the lives she has touched. There was the time when she gave me a large piece of lavender and silver brocade because she said lavender was "the most spiritual color." I feel myself privileged for those morning hours of counsel as we sat on a small balcony and read from the Bible, which I had known all my life, and from East Indian literature which I had not known…All I can say is that all of us – in the East – "touch her feet."[106]

Rare photograph of Martha Graham in A Florentine Madonna
photographed by Soichi Sunami. (Studies of Martha Graham.)
Courtesy of the Jerome Robbins Dance Division, The New York Public Library for the
Performing Arts, Special Collections, Astor, Lenox and Tilden Foundation.

Chapter 4

Martha Graham

Taurus, Born May 11, 1894

The true ruler of Taurus is kindly Mother Earth, a deity worshipped under many names. In Christendom, she has been replaced by the Madonna in her aspect of earth mother, the aspect in which she is pictorially represented as sheltering her children under a long flowing cloak. The Latin litany still chanted in her praise is said to include lines from an ancient hymn to Juno. The chief characteristic of the highly developed Taurean is her stability of character and purpose. Hers is the steadfast mind, unshaken in adversity, and the power of quiet persistence in the face of difficulties. She has found her true position with regard to the Universe, and that position is the *centre*. For them, there is always the inclination to hold settled convictions, one way or another, rather than to be swayed and harassed by difficulties. Taureans know what they believe and what they disbelieve, and have no objection to stating it if challenged. One of the dangers to their health is self-indulgence, particularly drunkenness.[1] Their natural vitality, always abundant, should be guided into proper channels, and given out freely and generously for the pleasure of others. Her sense of proportion is like the builder's instinct for what is really essential, emphasizing all that is good and permanent in the structure, and thereby adding greatly to the effect on the whole. She gives us no misshapen curves, no confused outlines. In forms of faith, in which the use of material, symbols – incense, rosaries, images and other physical aids, she finds great and solid concentration, based on solid foundations. These people believe in a future life and another world no doubt, but the claims of the physical plane, its uses and significance, are ever present on their minds. There is consequently some danger of idolatry – of exaltation of the relic or symbol of what is actually intended to be remembered.[2]

The way I try to illuminate or disturb or tell the truth as I see it is through dancing. Dancing to me is the revelation of the human being, good or bad, through movement. I try to explore the areas, the body and the soul of the human being. I am not a propagandist; I am an explorer; I am not a prophet; I hope I am a messenger.[3]

Complete sincerity of the body was Martha Graham's dictum from the early days of her dancing career. It was not only a belief, it was her commandment. In her first newspaper interview she told a reporter, "The only value of my work – if it has any art value – is absolute sincerity. I would not do anything that I couldn't feel. A dance must dominate me completely, until I lose sense of anything else."[4] In order to accurately understand the philosophies of Martha Graham, it is fitting to return to her early years when she was a small child growing up in Philadelphia.

Her father was an "alienist" – who specialized in treating people with disorders of the psyche. Dr. George Graham recognized his daughter's intelligence from an early age because she spent a great deal of time watching people in his office, reading his books, and asking many questions. He was an expert in detecting lying "by the manner in which people held their hands," and that observation of the link between personality and movement was not lost on Graham.

When I was very young, long before I started dancing, my father who was a surgeon for nervous disorders, taught me to look at people's movements as a key to their personalities. He taught me that movement never lies. A man's movements reveal his inner core.[5]

This was an important lesson in her evolution as a choreographer and dancer and that lesson of truth was a strong imprint for her spiritual philosophies. As a child during one of her haunts in her father's office, her primary lesson in how the body whispers truth was imparted to her, and this lesson would remain with her for the rest of her life. "He showed me a glass slide on which he had placed a drop of water. He held the slide in his hand between his thumb and index finger and said, 'Martha, what do you see?' I said, simply enough, 'Water.' And he said, 'Pure water?' I said, 'I think so. Pure water.' I thought my father was acting a bit strange and I did not know what he was getting at. Then, from a high shelf over his desk, he removed a microscope, I squinted one eye closed and brought the other to the heavy black lens. Then I saw the contents of the slide of water and said to my father in horror, 'But there are wriggles in it.' He said, 'Yes, it is impure. Just remember this all your life, Martha. You must look for the truth.' Look for the truth, whatever that truth may be – good, bad or unsettling."[6]

At age two, Graham's foray into the theatrical occurred when she "spontaneously lifted her skirts to flounce down a Presbyterian church aisle while her mother's head was bowed solemnly in prayer,"[7] much to the chagrin of her family. She pantomimed dances and her own choreographic ideas with her two sisters and their cook, Lizzie. The family moved from the East Coast to Santa Barbara when she was a pre-teenager, and at age thirteen she attended a concert of Ruth St. Denis and the Denishawn Dancers, a performance that would change her life. She was just two years shy of graduating high school, but at the end of the concert she *knew* that she wanted to devote her life to the dance. Her family wanted her to attend Vassar, but they compromised when they gave her permission to attend summer

Martha Speaks

I was born in Pittsburgh of Scotch-Irish parentage. My people were strict religionists who felt that dancing was sin. They frowned on all worldly pleasures, but were particularly horrified at my showing an early tendency toward an art that seemed grossly sensuous to them. My upbringing led me to fear it myself. But, California swung me in the direction of paganism, though years were to pass until I was fully emancipated. – NYMG-TFA, 62.

courses at Denishawn. When her father died while she was in high school, it allowed her the psychological freedom to pursue her passion for the dance, and once she graduated high school, she enrolled at the Denishawn School. What makes this story remarkable is the fact that Graham grew up in a community where dancing was considered not only trivial, it was *not allowed*. In fact, during that era, Ruth St. Denis's "Oriental" choreographic works depicting goddess figures were considered almost pagan.

Denishawn

Graham danced in a number of early Denishawn works, including *Dance of Egypt*, *Serenata Morisca*, *Danse Divertissements*, and *Garland Plastique* although it was her work in *Xochitl,* as the Indian priestess, that earned her the most acclaim during her years there.

Denishawn was an important stepping stone for her future, but, she soon became restless seeking to find her own way. In addition to her education and performance experiences at the school she met her ardent supporter, shoulder-to-cry on, mentor, and lover, musical director Louis Horst, who followed her and left Denishawn when she did. The pair were well suited, for both artists possessed talents that were years before their time. One of my favorite quotes by Horst is when he told Graham that she didn't have to worry about the music because she *was* the music.[8] It is even a higher compliment coming from a composer and musician of his stature. And he was correct, Graham's choreographic style came from the internal rhythms that pulsed through her.

The training at Denishawn was not only multifaceted it was revolutionary, and when one of her teachers sat on the floor to teach dance, offering a floor barre instead of the usual training that required bodies in an upright position, she witnessed another opportunity to think about how dance training could be. But her departure from Denishawn was necessary in the making of Graham as a serious dancer, in order for her unique choreographic style and technique to evolve. Struggling financially, she appeared in two seasons of the Greenwich Village Follies (dancing pseudo-Oriental Denishawn numbers), and retired temporarily from the stage to teach at the Eastman School in Rochester, New York. Employment at the school enabled her to have financial freedom so she could experiment with her ideas for dance technique; a technique that would not only revolutionize modern dance, but would earn her recognition as the founder of modern dance in the United States.

The Graham Technique

One of Martha Graham's glories of movement was her utilization and belief that the pelvic girdle was the form for seats of emotion. It was the birthplace, the link between the Above (Heaven) and Below (Earth), and what Graham called "the thing itself."[9] Graham's unique choreographic style and the Graham Technique was part of the training for "dislocations of the body," which could telegraph states of emotion, not merely descriptions of emotion. She knew that the body never lies, and her technique was a precise Rorsharch test of the body. "The fundamental form from which I started is movement. And I tried to develop the body as a pulse, a central vibration."[10] This central vibration in the center of the body is where the Graham Technique begins. She shared her disapproval of traditional ballet technique with Isadora Duncan, and both women maintained that ballet dancers were mistakenly using the body's center at the base of the spine in their training. Graham declared that the center of gravity lay in the pelvis and torso, and with that consciousness, the dancer's arms and legs would take care of themselves. Graham described her technique in an article written in 1941: "The first principle is the body center. The first movement is based upon the body in two acts of breathing – inhaling and exhaling – developing it from actual breathing experience to muscular activity independent of the actual act of breathing."[11]

This radical idea was the foundation for one of the greatest additions to dance. "Center" for Graham was a

Martha's Students Speak

If I were to tell you that she was an absolutely incandescent teacher at the time, it would be only words. But it was a fact that she set the students on fire; it was unbelievable. – Dorothy Bird, TNOMG, 48.

During rehearsals I watched Martha search within herself . . . Going with her into her search taught you a great deal about yourself. You could discover where your base was, that point within yourself where your energy is released into movement and dance. – May O'Donnell, TNOMG, 60.

I always felt the need to take class as an act of ritual. Martha Graham's creativeness is the body and soul of her technique. Her search deep within herself to objectify in terms of movement the inner life . . . brought discovery of movements that she needed to teach to her dancers. –Helen McGehee, TNOMG, 83.

From Martha's Journal

*"Such ecstasy, then, is an exalted form of contemplation.
Caught up in God (caught up in their vision)
I know it by experience."*
– St. Teresa, TNOMG, 20.

*What are the aspects of ecstasy –
Prayer – union with the Gods
Love – union with Mother
Divination, Hate, Faith.*
– TNOMG, 25.

*Man is all imagination. God is man & exists in us & we in him.
She who is entranced by visions.* – TNOMG, 26.

*Dance – as in trance.
Perhaps the dance is an ecstatic offering on all levels of experience to the act of life.*
– TNOMG, 27

triumvirate of the physical, emotional, and spiritual. Even as a child when she danced freely among the oak trees at a Sunday picnic, she was aware of what she was feeling in her body. "I stood on the table and began to dance. There was no music playing, but I still felt movement. Mother was embarrassed and made me stop."[12] Her intuitive abilities as well as her talents led her to not only create a new form of dance (modern dance), but to give her students over the years the permission to not only listen to their bodies, but to *honor* them.

This center is called *omphaloi*, or literally the navel.[13] The *omphalos* is considerably older than Christianity, dating back as far as 3000 BC in Egyptian culture. The "Center" is a spiritual reality and is of importance in all mysticism. Madame Blavatsky, a leader in esoteric teachings in the 1920s and 1930s, asserted that, "The ancients placed their astral soul of man, his-self-consciousness, in the pit of the stomach. The Brahmans shared this belief with Plato and other philosophers. The naval was regarded as 'the circle of the sun,' the seat of the divine eternal light. There exists the belief up to present day that adepts have a flame in their naval which enlightens to them all darkness and discloses the spiritual world as well as things unseen."[14]

The Center is what Plato called a divine idea of form and what St. Augustine referred to as an archetype. "There is no sacred site, symbol or image which can contain or reveal the total power and significance of the Center. The sites and symbols of the Center are merely nodes, gateways, giving access to something that is otherwise inaccessible."[15]

Graham's classes were full of mystical illusions: "In dance, each time it may be a mystical or religious connotation that you feel, but principally it is the body exalting in its strength and its own power."[16] As a dancer myself, I can't imagine a more potent declaration.

To educate her "entire being," Graham read voraciously during her life and her notebooks testify to this.[17] The notebooks are full of references to books written by such authors

*"Ritual Dancer" by artist Kim Goldfarb
inspired by a piece of driftwood found by the artist.*

*She not only used our bodies,
she also used our inner lives,
she co-opted our souls.
– Mark Ryder, TNOMG, 81.*

*She was a sorceress, you know
in the Irish sense of having
insight and being able to command people to do her bid-
ding. She has superhuman
power. In the studio . . . no
one else existed for you or for
her. She was the enchantress in
the situation. Half of the time
I didn't know what the hell she
was talking about – it was so
mystical and spiritual. – John
Butler, TNOMG, 87.*

*Technique is important, but
soul is more important. You
have to project what you feel.
If that is not there, the technique is empty and does not
really matter. While Martha
has physical gifts, and developed her technique, she also
developed her soul. – Takako
Asakawa, TNOMG, 126.*

as Evelyn Underhill (on mysticism), Joseph Campbell (myth), Mircea Eliade (shamanism), and Coomaraswamy (nature, mysticism, Zen, etc.). She also read philosophers, dramatists, novelists and poets, quoted the Bible, chapter and verse, and spent some time in analysis with a Jungian therapist, who no doubt influenced her reading choices. Books were as sacred to her as her choreography was: "I have a holy attitude towards books. If I was stranded on a desert island, I'd need only two: the dictionary and the Bible."[18]

Her mystical understandings were extensive, as was her habit of writing favorite quotations in her notebooks. Many of these sources she used as sources for inspiration for her choreography.

Graham wanted to create a system of movement for dance that had never existed before, a system that she hoped "people would bow down before some day." "The instrument of dance is the human body; the medium of movement. The body has always been to me a thrilling wonder, a dynamo of energy, exciting, courageous, powerful; a delicately balanced logic and proportion. It has not been my aim to evolve or discover a new method of dance training, but rather to dance significantly. To dance significantly means through the medium of discipline and by means of a sensitive, strong instrument to bring into focus unhackneyed movement; a human being."[19]

In tandem with her choreographic choices consisting of contractions, release, and spiral (the basis of her technique), "Graham invented a dance vocabulary of angular lines, a system of leverages, balances, and dynamics of stunningly abrupt falls to the ground. It looked explosive; torsos were clenched, then released; bodies coiled on the floor, dancers spiraled upward from a kneeling stance, and focused all attention on the torso."[20] This signature style was the style of yoga, which shared the same attention to breath/release and focus on the inner body.

Ballet by its very form demands that the dancer move fluidly, always striving to conceal effort. Graham believed that this effort was vital, and because effort begins with the nerve centers, a technique developed from percussive impulses that flow through the body, the arms and legs would have enormous vitality. She termed these impulses, "contractions." These contractions and their subsequent release would be where the dancer could find center, because center is the place hollowed out in the depths of the abdominal wall. Agnes De Mille, a legendary dancer and choreographer in her own right, believed that Graham's contributions to the dance were "probably the greatest addition to dance vocabulary that has been made in this century, comparable to the rules of perspective in painting."[21]

What is so extraordinary about Graham's work as an artist and educator is her idea of the *living spirit* of the emotions that arise in the dancer's body without any theatric ality or pretense. This idea of no pretensions, where the body is clear and honest, is Graham's extraordinary gift to dancers of our time. She was not afraid to show all emotions: negative, ugly, constricting, often stark and hard-to-watch, in a time when most audiences were seeking to be merely entertained. In the words of one of her students, "She wanted to say something in terms of movement. It was like she was stepping out of this encasement of Denishawn. She wanted to move the body differently. And she certainly did. The first movements she worked on were the 'Graham falls.' It was percussive – it was as though someone hit you, and you went back and fell. You were using the contraction when you got hit and fell. When you came up, you came up with your entire body naturally, not like a toe-dancer who came up with prettiness and beauty."[22]

Discipline

Discipline is one of the most integral components in living as a dancer, whether one appears on the stage or not. When one has made the choice and commitment to dance, the art form requires steadfast dedication, time, and discipline of the body. Even when Graham couldn't dance anymore, she hadn't lost her internal passion for movement. Demonstrating class while seated in a chair, she felt that "the movement comes from my own body. I don't get up and do leaps across the room, but my body never stops moving when I'm directing…There is a tumbling inside of me, a desire to move…"[23]

Often speaking about the discipline required to become a dancer and how that discipline was part and parcel of living an authentic life, ideas that one usually finds in mystical and philosophical literature, Graham explained that, "Training, technique, is important; but it is always in the artist's mind only the means to an end. Its importance is that it frees the body to become its *ultimate self.* Training and technique are means to strength, to freedom, to spontaneity…A program of physical activity which involves only

Martha Speaks

I used to work by myself. I just wanted to find out what the body was capable of doing. Then, I'd try out movements on my pupils. Gradually a system evolved. It didn't evolve from a theory, but from practice. The theory comes later, and the documentation, the analysis, the correction, the elimination of things. You have to have terrific energy. If you're able to stand the impact of that energy, then you can express more than another person can perhaps. You have to have a very strong body – a dancer does – disciplined well, with the right conformation. You have to submit to your calling and work like the devil to make a craft. If you do that, the chances are that something will come through you. And it only comes through you if you have a language – movement or speech – some means of communicating. – MGF, 2-3.

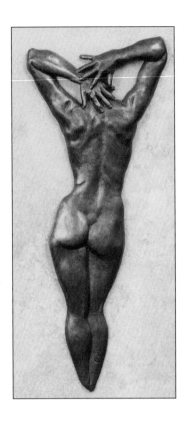

*The female torso beautifully
sculpted by artist Kelly Borsheim.*

exercises for strength, and a means of emotional catharsis, through so called 'self-expression dancing' will never produce a complete human being…The puritanical concept of life has always ignored the fact that the nervous system and the body as well as the mind are involved in experience, and art cannot be experienced except by one's entire being."[24]

The Divine Energy and the Breath of God

Her teaching style was also unusual, utilizing the breath with contractions, and certainly this interchange of energies, was the "the letting out and the taking in of life energy," another important imprint of yoga. Former Graham dancer Bertram Ross affirmed, "Martha said that you must drain yourself to take something in."[25] This awareness of the body and breath is similar to Eastern religious meditation techniques because the breath has always been the foundation for achieving higher states of consciousness. In Sanskrit, two energy channels play particularly important roles in the body; *ida* and *pingala*. "Ida is the carrier of cool and calming energy. Its channel begins left of the root chakra [in the lower pelvis] and ends in the left nostril. Pingala functions as a carrier of the solar energy, which is full of heat and drive. This channel begins on the right hand side of the root chakra and ends in the upper area of the right nostril." [26] Both the ida and pingala are able to transmute vital life energies or *prana* directly from the air. As the dancers expel their breath, they are also discharging toxins from their bodies of both physical and emotional content.

Graham's technique was the form in which these vital and divine energies could be tapped, not only on stage, but while dancing at the studio in rehearsals. When she and the dancers engaged in these exercises, they were also sending energies into their bodies, not only for increased vitality, but for self-healing. This continual interplay between the outward movement process and the inward awareness of the body was one of the keys to her training. Graham's inner life and understanding was so evolved that she was able to develop true insight from her own center, her own core, and by attunement to her breath.

> I see what the body does when it breathes. When it breathes in, it is a release and when it breathes out, it is a contraction. It's the physical use of the body in action. My technique is based on breathing. I have based everything that I have done on the pulsation of life, which is, to me, the pulsation of breath. Every time you breathe life or expel it, it is a

Martha Speaks

My sister Lizzie began to take me to the Mission in Santa Barbara, which was called the Queen of the Missions. Founded by the Franciscan Fathers, it was the most beautiful of the Southern California Missions. I remember how the Sisters of St. Clare, devout followers of the ways of Francis, would lie prone in prayer in front of the altar. Something of the sunlight and the color of the stone permeated the service[s] and gave it a kind of livingness. – BM, 49.

release or a contraction. It is that basic to the body. You are born with these two movements and you keep both until you die. But you begin to use them consciously so that they are beneficial to the dance dramatically. You must animate that energy within yourself. It animated the world and everything in it. I recognized early in my life that there was this kind of energy, some animating spark, or whatever you choose to call it. It can be Buddha, it can be anything, it can be everything. It begins with breath. I am sure that levitation is possible. I am not speaking mystically, I am speaking practically. I am sure that I could walk in the air, but my heart is not trained to stand the urgency of that flight, the movement that comes up through and rests against the heart.[27]

When Graham speaks about the "animating spark" she is referring to the energies that rest inside the body in sacred space, and her knowledge about the mystical aspects of dance were notable. When she was a young girl, her visits to the missions of California with her sisters made a deep impression upon her, and these inspirations appear in many of her works in honor of the Virgin and other goddess figures.

The ancient philosopher Gregory of Palamas spoke of the transformed vision of those who have been "deified" or "divinized." Graham knew that she was one of those persons. "Miraculously, they see with a sense that exceeds the senses, and with a mind that exceeds mind," the philosopher noted, "for the power of the spirit penetrates their human faculties, and allows them to see things that are beyond us."[28] Graham seemed able to understand intuitively the power of that spiritual energy and was able to employ the transformation of those energies not only within her own body, but in the bodies of her dancers through training.

Palamas also wrote of the ability of the spiritual man (in this case, the spiritual woman) "'through the grace of the Spirit, transmitted to the body through the soul, grants to the body the experience of things divine.' [Graham's] understanding ties in with the esoteric doctrine of the 'centers,' which teaches the significance of certain areas of the body as focal points for occult and spiritual energies."[29] She was using the focal points of breath, of contraction and release, and embodiment of the life force itself for that transmutation. Her mystical teachings were often cryptic. Referring to the spine as the "Divine Tree of Life," it is clear that Graham studied the sacred mystical teaching of the Kabbalah, which was symbolically depicted as a tree.

Graham often kept her hands closed in her performances enabling her to contain the energies of her body; "She never opens her hands but closed [them] in believing that this retained energy – it doesn't flow out indiscriminately – it flows back to her."[30] Ancient mystery schools have always maintained that the more highly evolved a human being was, the more they have embodied their true potential. This potential, in this particular form, *through* the body was knowledge in which Graham was quite educated. Her notebooks, interviews with former students, and testimonies of dance critics all witness to something quite spiritual about Martha Graham. She knew that "the shamans, the holy men of the past are the artists of today," and through her dance contributions, she became a *curandera*, a healer who used movement instead of herbs as a prescription for health and healing. The concept of *kundalini* rising, a Hindu description of the movement of divine life force up the spine, was familiar to Graham, as was the understanding of the charkas, the subtle energy vortexes in the body.

According to healer and metaphysician Rosalyn L. Bruyere, "Each of the seven traditional chakras has a physical, an emotional, a creative, and a celestial component. Each chakra has its own purpose or particular viewpoint based upon the area of consciousness that it influences. The ancient yogis as well as the ancient Egyptians and Greeks called this component a *body*. This body is simply an area or realm of existing or potential consciousness."[31]

Martha Speaks

The body never lies. The body is a very strange business. The chakras awake the center of energy in the body, as in kundalini yoga. The awakening starts in the feet and goes up. Through the torso, the neck, up, up, through the head, all the while releasing energy.
– BM, 122.

Graham understood this philosophy, and her technique was specifically designed not only to align the chakras for optimal physical health, but to awaken higher spiritual vibrations in the body for spiritual well being, even bliss states. Transformation to a higher vibration can occur with kundalini awakenings through the spine since, as Swami Kriyananda (a direct disciple of the great Indian master Paramhansa Yogananda) explains, "the spine is a corridor containing a succession of locked doors: chakras, it would be well to add that the same key fits all these doors. This key is the energy as it rises toward the brain through the spine, passing along the sushumna or nerve channel and stimulating the chakras. The energy's passage through each of these doors awakens one to a new level of spiritual awareness and a heightened sense of well-being. It is as though, with its awakening, each chakra dropped a veil that had been obscuring the ego's awareness. When electricity passes through a wire [a body], it generates a magnetic field. This field is spiral. The same thing happens when the energy moves through the body, particularly in its ascent in the spine. The magnetism generated is spiritual rather than physical…spiral in movement."[32] This spiral form of energy or movement is one of Graham's inscriptions. Her innate understanding of the tenets of metaphysical thought and Eastern religions dominated her technique, yet, sparse documentation of that understanding is published.

Graham's technique classes utilizing deep breathing exercises were also training ground for the arousal of the kundalini energies when one considers that "the breath in the body goes way down from the genitals up through the waist, through the throat, and through the top of the head, and then down again…The dancer works from the base of the spine all the way through the center of the body, the navel, the heart, the mouth, the head…The Force comes through the center of the body and finally bursts out."[33] She was not only aware of this energy which can be a strong

*Isadora Duncan Study by Abraham Walkowitz. Pen and Ink. n.d.
(ca. 1925-1930.) Courtesy of University Gallery, University of
Delaware, Gift of Virginia Zabriskie.*

healing force, but it also was possible to have a kundalini
experience using her techniques.

> No one invents movement, movement is discovered.
> There is only one law of posture that I have been
> able to discover – the perpendicular line connecting
> Heaven and Earth. It is possible and wise to teach
> these exercises even to the person who has no desire
> to dance professionally. It must be emphasized that
> performance of these exercises is not a mere matter

of having a good time, but of achieving a center of body and mind which will eventually, but not immediately result in a singing freedom – because power means to become what one is, to the highest degree of realization.[34]

Graham's intuitive awareness of "achieving a center of body and mind" (*see* sidebar) is based on the spiritual philosophy of being in the present, or in the now. This was not a new-agenotion, but a foundational principle of all spiritual beliefs. "Be still and know that I am God," found in the Psalms suggests that through quieting the mind and aligning with ourselves, ("achieving a center of body and mind") one can not only know oneself, but know the presence of the Divine within. Buddhists call this process *samantha* (to stop), and *vipasyana* (looking deeply). The mystic scholar, Thich Nhat Hanh, writes about his earliest practice of breathing to achieve this alignment of being totally present through the breath, in his book, *Living Buddha, Living Christ*. His description echoes Graham's technique for breath work with her dancers.

> The first practice I learned as a novice monk was to breathe in and out consciously, to touch each breath with my mindfulness, identifying the in-breath as in-breath and the out-breath as out-breath. When you practice this way, *your mind and body come into alignment, your wandering thoughts come to a stop, and you are at your best.* Mindfulness is the substance of a Buddha.[35]

Graham was a close friend of the philosopher and mythic writer Joseph Campbell, who was married to one of her dancers, Jean Erdman. Once she screamed to Campbell backstage before a performance, "Wait till I get up on the Kundalini."[36] This was a woman who was fully versed in and aware of the powers of the metaphysical body. She clearly

Martha Speaks

In life, heightened nerve sensitivity produces that concentration on the instant which is true living. In dance, this sensitivity produces action timed to the present moment. It is the result of a technique for the revelation of experience. To me, this acquirement of nervous, physical, and emotional concentration is the one element possessed to the highest degree by the truly great dancers of the world. Its acquirement is the result of discipline, of energy in the deep sense. That is why there are so few great dancers." – MDP.

studied the ancient teachings of kundalini rising, intuitively understood those teachings, and *created breathing exercises* for her students to awaken these energies. Frequently asking her students to pay attention to the energies within their bodies [while experiencing the contraction and release], she was actually resurrecting the tenets of kundalini rising in ancient texts using: breath, movement, concentration, and awareness. She never took credit for inventing a new form of movement, but said that she "simply rediscovered what the body can do," which further validates this theory.

The emphasis on the breath would have been her own masking of awakening kundalini, since these energies encompass the pelvis and the seat of the spine, and begin in the lower trunk and rise up inside the body. Ironically, perhaps Graham chose not to speak about these subtle-body energies in great depth, not because she was afraid to do so, but because historically, sacred practitioners in mystery schools were sworn to secrecy about their contacts into the higher worlds. Certainly, that taboo remains today for people who choose a mystical path.

The Virgin Mary

Graham created more than two hundred choreographic works with many themes of goddess figures, as well as saints, angels, and the Madonna. These religious ideals were firmly embedded in her creative mind. During seventy years of performing and choreographing she specifically made three choreographic works in honor of the Virgin Mary. [37] Her first dance to honor the Madonna, entitled *From a XII-Century Tapestry,* premiered April 18, 1926, at the 48th Street Theater in New York. On May 27 of that year, she performed the same concert and retitled it, *A Florentine Madonna.* Short of cash, she enlisted the aid of Frances Steloff, the proprietor of the famous Gotham Book Mart. Steloff used to give Graham books when she could not afford to pay for them, and although Graham believed she was a "nobody," Steloff loaned her one thousand dollars.

Her second work, called *Madonna* (originally named *Adagio*) was presented on October 16, 1927, at The Little Theater in New York; and her third, *Primitive Mysteries*, followed on February 2, 1931 at the Craig Theater also in New York. The latter is considered, among dance scholars, as one of her most important works.

I have found no reviews of her first two Madonna pieces. However, considering that she also appeared again as the Madonna in a full-length theatrical play/dance, these works together provide compelling insights into the first appearances on stage of Martha Graham as a dancer. Her earliest work on stage was often derivative of her Denishawn days, because she had not fully developed her unique style. The fact that she would choose to perform *any* Madonna dance in the beginning of her career is mysterious because she was not a religious person in the sense of formal religion, yet she was a deeply spiritual woman. In all of the books, journals, letters, and other research that I have done, including contemporary commentary on her work, these[38] particular dances aren't discussed, perhaps because they aren't considered important works, or perhaps they were too "Denishawn like." But the earliest Madonna choreographies are important in the sense that they paved the way for her choreography in *Primitive Mysteries* and in *El Penitente* – two major works.

Although the answers to why she choose the Madonna, a divine being, to depict at the beginning of her career are illusive, I believe she offered many clues. It is quite revelatory that when Martha Graham penned her autobiography, which was published the year of her death in 1991 at age ninety-seven, she chose a cryptic quote for the Epigraph that tells us much about Graham's obvious connection to the Divine. The quote is obscure, taken from the Proto Evangelium[39] of Jacobi (also called James), written in the second century AD. It is also fitting. The quote reads: "And the lot of the purple and the scarlet fell to Mary."[40]

In asking why Graham chose to identify with the Virgin Mary as a woman and artist, it is important to understand the full reference from which this quote is sourced.

Now, there was a council of priests, and they said: Let us make a veil for the temple of the Lord. And the priest said: Call unto me pure virgins…And the priests called to mind the child Mary, that she was of the tribe of David and was undefiled before God: and the priest said: Cast me lots, which of you shall weave the gold and the undefiled (the white) and tile fine linen and the silk and the hyachinthine, and the scarlet and the true purple. *And the lot of the true purple fell unto Mary*, and she took them and went unto her house.

And Mary took the scarlet and began to spin it. And she took the pitcher and went forth to fill it with water: and lo a voice saying: Hail, thou that art highly favored; the Lord is with thee: blessed art thou among women…and took the purple and sat down upon her seat and drew out the thread. And behold the angel of the Lord stood before her saying; Fear not, Mary, for thou hast found grace before the Lord of all things, and thou shalt conceive of his word. And she, when she heard it, questioned in herself, saying, Shall I verily conceive of the living God, and bring forth after the manner of all woman? And the angel of the Lord said: Not so, Mary, for a power of the Lord shall overshadow thee: and wherefore also that holy thing which shall be born of thee shall be called the Son of the Highest. And thou shalt call his name Jesus…And she made the purple and the scarlet and brought them unto the priest. And the priest blessed her and said: Mary, the Lord God hath magnified thy name,

Martha Speaks

Art always has a relationship to the Spirit in creating it and appreciating it as something through which one enters the spiritual world. Yet one cannot be an artist without giving one's own creation an objective existence, so that it lives in the world, which one is also considering from a spiritual point of view. If one forgets that spiritual relationship, art goes through a transformation, and changes more or less into non-art. – CRS, 171-172.

and thou shalt be blessed among all generations of the earth.[41]

Graham frequently entered the spiritual world not only to create her dances, but when she was performing. The attributes of the colors purple and scarlet, are interesting to examine because both are referred to as colors of the divine, and the significance of those colors were apparent to her.

Purple: Purple is the color of the magisterium. It is a color combining blue (spirituality and nobility), and red, (courage and virility), and symbolizes knowledge, religious devotion, the colors of the goddess of the Dawn, and love of truth. It stands for the foundation of the Kabbalah, and possesses of all other colors the highest frequency. Purple has always possessed an air of authority, majesty as well as mystery.[42]

Scarlet: Scarlet is the symbol of the Mystic Borderland and symbolizes spiritual attainment and self-mastery, wisdom and saintliness.[43]

The Virgin Mary and Martha Graham had several common threads in their lives. Graham identified with Mary's sacred mission, although each would follow different paths. Mary, the Madonna, would give birth to Jesus, and Graham would give birth to her dances. Two particular lines in the works are worth pondering. The first is, *"for a power of the Lord shall overshadow thee."* The second is, *"the Lord God hath magnified thy name, and thou shalt be blessed among all generations of earth."* Graham considered herself a sacred instrument and that, in her case, the instrument was her body. She often made references to dancers as "athletes of God," and "servants of the soul." The second line has even greater significance when one considers that Graham chose this significant quote at the end of her life, when she had

Martha Graham as the Madonna. Photography by Soichi Sunami. (Studies of Martha Graham.) Courtesy of the Jerome Robbins Dance Division, The New York Public Library for the Performing Arts, Special Collections, Astor, Lenox and Tilden Foundation.

time to reflect on her life's journey. Graham also reveals her spiritual focus as she wrote in her notebooks; "Thus may my divine mission be crowned with success, and may I attain to the body of glory," adding, "Psychic Energy 391 (a little known Tibetan ritual by means of which the yogin seeks to transcend ego-consciousness & attain to consciousness of the Self)." [44]

Graham received numerous awards, including the U.S. Presidential Medal of Freedom, for her accomplishments during her lifetime; she was also named an artistic emissary for the United States abroad, and was the first dancer to perform at the White House. But, those crowns of success are probably not what Graham was referring to in characterizing her life. I believe that Graham knew that she was blessed, that *God had magnified her name* in dance, and that she was also *blessed among all generations*[45] of the earth. While it would have been a lofty and even ego maniacal point of view to compare herself with the Mother of God, Graham could genuinely acknowledge that she too received the "lot of purple and scarlet" in her own life. Considering her enormous repertoire of creations that possess a spiritual theme – *Acrobats of God, Adorations, Diversion of Angels, Eyes of the Goddess, Judith, Lucifer, Out of This World, The Plain of Prayer, Primitive Mysteries, Madonna* (all forms), *Seraphic Dialogue, Triumph of St. Joan*, and *Visionary Recital* – this idea has even more credence.

Rudolph Steiner believed that, "When Rafael painted Madonnas there was a deeper reason for this. The essence of the Madonna lived in human hearts and souls and – in the noblest sense – something came from the soul of the masses that could join with this creation."[46] Graham knew that the Madonna was alive in her and that the soul of the masses (in her audiences) would be able to join in this understanding, even on a primitive level.

Former Graham dancer Gertrude Schurr witnessed her performance as the Madonna and remarked that the concert was "so beautiful that I cried."[47] On October 16, 1927,

Agnes De Mille once asked Graham if she ever got depressed. "All the time,"
[Martha] replied brightly. "But I never tell."
In 1976, when the President of the United States hung the Medal of Freedom around Martha's neck, it was not for a single act of valor or a single dance. It was for the days and hours and years of walking, stretching, rolling, thinking, praying and
dropping to rest. And for being steadfast. Martha was our North Star." –Agnes De Mille, MAR, 266.

Graham danced *Adagio* (later retitled *Madonna)* at The Little Theatre in New York City. On the program, she performed *Revolt*, which is mentioned in reviews, a piece that Fanny Brice later spoofed in her sketch at the Ziegfield Follies calling it "Rewolt."[48]

Her Underworld Journey

Graham frequently received negative comments even from those close to her, and it must have hurt her. In the beginning of her career, the influence of her teachers, Ruth St. Denis and Ted Shawn, remained. "I did many dances, and everything I did was influenced by Denishawn. There was an audience. They came because I was such a curiosity – a woman who could do her own work."[49]After her first solo performance in 1926 – when she danced solos to the music of Schumann, Debussy, Ravel, and other composers – a friend of Ruth St. Denis, her former teacher, came backstage and told her, "Martha, this is simply dreadful. How long do you expect to keep it up?" Graham replied, "As long as I've got an audience."[50]

Years later, even Graham's mother joined in her disapproval, telling her, "Martha, I don't see why you have to present such dreadful women on the stage. You're really rather sweet when you're at home." Graham felt that "some didn't want me to get ahead. They thought I was extremely ugly and did dreadful things."[51] The *New York Times* gave a brief mention of her "interpretive dance to modern music,"[52] while her former mentors, St. Denis and Shawn collected negative reviews and sent them with a letter advising her that "she was going in the wrong direction, wasting her time and resources, and that she has made a profound mistake in leaving Denishawn."[53]

However, Graham's fervent belief in herself motivated her to persevere, and it ultimately didn't matter to her whether she was supported or understood. But, she must have known that her originality was disturbing to people. This originality is often a plight for many artists and visionaries, and similar vilification continues even in present day. Lincoln Kirstein, a scholar (and the man responsible for bringing genius George Balanchine to New York), summed it up perfectly: "Graham's contribution is unique and uniquely personal. I have always felt one of her most difficult characteristics was her frightening originality, her independence of any tradition whatsoever; but like [William] Blake, she has had to create her 'own system or be enslaved by another man's.' But her sense of a projected physicality, her spinal integration, her sense of controlled entrances, and the deep human color of her dancing style, is a purer and frequently deeper repository of essential classicism, even if it may be a narrower one than the easily accepted and much more superficial idiom of school-ballet."[54]

Graham knew she was a "heretic," "a woman who is put upon in all she does, a woman who is frightened. Every place she goes she goes against the heavy beat and footsteps of all she opposes. Maybe she is a heretic in a religious way, maybe in a social way. I felt at the time that I was a heretic. I was outside the realm of women. I did not dance the way that people danced…In many ways I showed onstage what most people came to the theatre to avoid."[55] She knew that she possessed a unique calling, one that would grant her many hours of discontent and loneliness, and even drove her to drink excessively. Graham recognized her dream world as a potent and powerful creative inspiration and relied on her intuitive abilities at all costs, valuing its wisdom. "If you have not destroyed your intuitive acceptance and recognition of things, you have a chance. Of course, if you have destroyed that intuitive thing, you are finished."[56]

Graham had her share of criticism from friends and family, critics, and arts organizations. Her application to participate in the first Federal (U.S.) exchange program with Russia was refused because she was a "disturbing influence on the young." Shattered by the dissolution of her marriage to fellow dancer Erick Hawkins, Graham's personal pain was reflected in one of her journal entries after he left her.

Martha Speaks

There is wonderful Icelandic term: "doom eager." You are doom eager for destiny no matter what it costs you. The ordeal of isolation, the ordeal of loneliness, the ordeal of doubt, the ordeal of vulnerability which it takes to compose in any medium, is hard to face. – CWMG, 118.

I know it was the bite
of these empty, hungry hours
that now devour me, beloved
when I sometimes caught your sleeve.[57]

She even entertained the idea of adopting a young Indian child she wanted to name, Ericka, and she said it was the "most vivid reality " she had "regarding a child, the most complete identification of her life "with one of a child's." Yet, she never proceeded with the adoption.

Graham's work with her a Jungian therapist, Mrs. Frances Wickes, offered to her not only a deep friendship, but a sacred encounter where she would explore freely her life, her ideas, and her despair without censure. However, after one meeting, Mrs. Wickes lectured her on her arrogance and told her, "Martha, you are not a goddess, you must admit your mortality."[58] In a letter to Wickes in 1952, she gives voice to her feelings of despair that she is experiencing in this time of her life and the letter is written with an acceptance of faith and trust, two elements that are integral in the mystic's journey.

I am not dire. I may be stuck or think I am but not that I am in the misery I was even at this time last year. The only real difference is that now there seems to be no hope. I cannot even say that there is none. Hope is a corrupting, corroding thing. It is, I suppose, a thing of personal will. Faith seems an acceptance of a larger view of things and a less accented personal attitude. Faith is necessary and hope is not.

Primitive Mysteries

In 1931, Graham choreographed *Primitive Mysteries*, considered to be one of her most enduring and important works. It is a powerful dance of women, all women, who gather around Graham as the Madonna figure.[59]

In order to understand the evolution of this piece, it is important to cite contributing factors that influenced her creative sensibility. During the previous three years, Graham's lover, Horst, continued to be her guiding light, inspiration, "a rock" even though she accused him of "trying to break her." He recognized her genius and potential even before she had found her path. "He helped her to release what she later called 'divine discontent' in a torrent of creative energy."[60] Her advocate, he wrote a letter to St. Denis when she danced as the Madonna: "She did one thing to a sacred song in a Madonna costume that opened like your Quan Yin, and progressed through many religious poses – quite beautiful."[61]

Frequent traveling companions, Graham and Horst traveled to Santa Barbara, California, to visit her mother, who had remarried after her father's death. It was to be a restorative journey after an intense time of performing and creating. The pair chose to drive through the Southwest upon their return. In 1930, they stayed at a cottage near Santa Fe, where she would witness her inspiration for *Primitive Mysteries*. They attended several Native American sacred dance ceremonies including the corn ceremony at the Jemez Pueblo, the sunset dance at the Picuris Pueblo, the corn dances at the Santa Clara Pueblo, and the ceremonial dances at the Zia Pueblo. *Pueblo* is the Spanish word for "people" or "village," and Graham's visits to many different pueblos during her life affected her deeply as an artist and choreographer. These dances not only ritualized the honoring of the Creator for its blessings, but they were also an opportunity to bring the entire village together in unison.

During this trip, Graham and Horst also spent some time with writer Mabel Dodge Luhan.[62] Graham had read Luhan's article in the *Theatre Arts Monthly* entitled "A Bridge Between Two Cultures," in which she called to "the nation's creative geniuses to save themselves and Western civiliza-

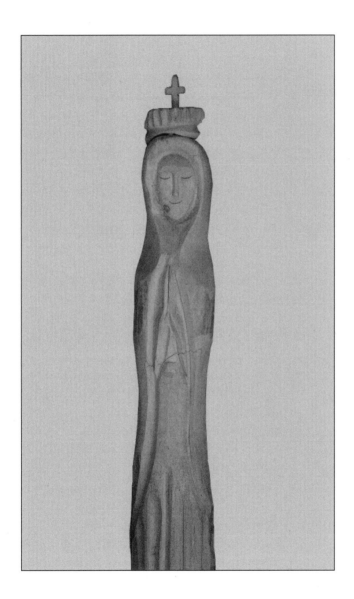

An unusual wooden depiction of the Virgin Mary
taken by photographer Mark Roseman.

tion…she compared modern-day artists to the ancient Romans, claiming that they were foredoomed to perish because of their pandering to commercialism."[63] Luhan also exhorted artists to champion and return to the "static virtues of truth, beauty and the eternal."[64] Like Graham, Luhan drew inspiration from the landscape of the Southwest and the Indian way of life, honoring the earth and the Creator. "Out of a reverence for the soil and the wonder of fertility have grown these great rituals of the American Indian. And linked with these, the mysteries of propagation and of the fiery energies of the human soul and its transferable power have blended and fused into the pattern of existence that is at the same time both life and art. For with the Indians life is art – and religion is its testimony." [65]

In New Mexico also the pair visited the religious sect of the Penitentes in the Sangre de Cristo mountains, a sect that fascinated them.[66] Los Hermanos Penitentes, or the Brotherhood of the Penitents, lived in all but complete. Their practice of self-flagellation, "who whipped themselves bloody as they sought to rekindle their own compassion and redeem humanity by sharing in the suffering of Christ,"[67] was not embraced by clergy or the public, and hence their isolation. What transpired during Graham's visit is not recorded, however, the impression of that first trip to New Mexico would have lasting effects.

In New Mexico to "'know the land'…from it will come the great mass drama that is the American Dance,"[68] Graham wrote in a letter to a friend, adding that the first night she arrived, she saw a Navajo blanket woven in natural colors of sheep – white, brown, and black – in stripes. Two crosses at each end were in red, signifying crossroads. "It was very prophetic – I was at the crossroads." [69] She also included in her note a vivid description of the dance ceremony at the Santo Domingo Pueblo. The dance was a corn dance, fittingly performed on the feast day of Saint Dominic, a monk who believed that both the body and the spirit were intrinsically good. Given Graham's early child-

About the Dances of the Pueblo Indians

"The Pueblo peoples are well known for their beautiful religious dances. These are intended to reciprocate for blessings, especially the rain and snow, and to express human responsibility for maintaining balance and peace in the world. Whether a dancer or an observer, everyone present at a dance endeavors to be grateful, humble, and serene so that their good thoughts and kindly intentions will mingle into a powerful prayer for the welfare of all mankind." – PAM, 6.

hood in which dancing was not allowed and the body was not encouraged to move freely, this dance had a profound effect.

The Native American's earnestness, complete focus, and purpose in the sacred act of dancing were clear to Graham when she created *Primitive Mysteries*. When she performed *Mysteries* the company received an unprecedented *twenty-three* curtain calls. John Martin, the critic for the *New York Times*, one of the most articulate and intelligent reviewers of his day, wrote:

> Miss Graham is a pronounced radical, an individualist to the last degree in her artistic convictions, and one finds compromise the most difficult thing to approach when the principles for which she stands are involved…She has already touched the borderland of that mystic territory where greatness dwells. That she has not received the accolade from the general public cannot be explained altogether by the fact that she has sometimes missed the ultimate perfection in her art…At the conclusion of her "Primitive Mysteries"…the majority of the house burst into cheers. It was not just a scattering of "bravo's",…but was the expression of a mass of people whose emotional tension found spontaneous release. Here is the composition which must be ranked among the choreographic masterpieces of the modern dance movement.[70]

Martin knew that Graham's work was an acquired taste, and just two years earlier he wrote in his column in the *Times*, "She does the unforgivable thing for a dancer to do – She makes you think; yet it is thinking of a peculiar character, for it is less of the brain than of some organ absent from anatomical charts, that reacts to esthetic stimulation…There is no pretense about Martha Graham, no concession to popularity, no deliberate courting of sensational-

Martha Speaks

I arrived when they were dancing. I heard their voices and I rounded the corner of an adobe house in a narrow street, to enter the plaza – and saw them – one hundred men in a straight line – dancing and chanting. The chanting was low, deep, intense. The faces of the men pure and fanatical and beautiful as gods. They danced in perfect unison – for no one. They danced to generate the magic for rain, good crops, and fertile land and people. There were about six visitors that was all. It is difficult to describe – but nothing I have ever seen or dreamed of equaled that great communal dance ritual in earnestness, intensity, faith in the eternal recurrence of natural phenomena – such savage ruthless awareness of life. It was the most pure holy ceremony. There was not only great soul – but the sense of form was also moving. They are so wise and such great artists. – LH, 100.

ism. You can take her or leave her, but you cannot divert that fixed gaze which looks so intently ahead into a world which is completely hers to explore."[71]

The intelligence of both mind and body was not the usual fare for audiences and explains why Graham was not always received with open arms. One critic was barred from her performances, although he managed to sneak inside in defiance. Mary Watkins, one of the first salaried dance critics and the writer for the *New York Herald Tribune* (and also *Denishawn Magazine*), understood her work and wrote about the religious fervor that surrounded *Primitive Mysteries.*

> Miss Graham is generally acknowledged as the leader of the moderns…and it must be admitted that she baffles and perplexes almost as many as she inspires. Even the most uninitiated, who are left completely cold by the Graham manifestations will grant her a certain amount of respect. Even if he cannot understand, the layman recognized that here is an artist who knows where she is going, who has firm grip upon something which is vital and contemporary…By some mysterious alchemy known only to herself, Miss Graham combines her asceticism, her satire, her perverseness into a pungent and salty whole which bears the unmistakable hallmark of genius. This work is the most significant choreography which has yet come out of America. It is a masterpiece of construction, but it achieves a mood which actually lifts both spectators and dancers to rarefied heights of *spiritual ecstasy.*[72]

The ritualistic and spiritual connotations of *Primitive Mysteries* compare with *yugen*, the Japanese term for mysteries of profound beauty. "Yugen is a compound word, each part, yu and gen, meaning cloudy impenetrability and the combination meaning obscurity, unknowability, and mystery, beyond intellectual calculation. It is something we feel within ourselves and yet is an object of mutual communication among those who have a feeling for it. It is hidden behind the clouds, but not entirely out of sight, for we feel its presence."[73] This concept (of yugen), which was very much alive in Graham's choreography, is also akin to the mystical experience which is hidden, and yet we feel its presence; a presence remarkably translated to Graham's audience through visceral receivership by the audience members.

Little did the reviewers know that Graham had spent the night before the performance sleeping in her dressing room, doubting herself and thinking that *Primitive Mysteries* would be a complete failure. It's a majestic piece, which not only transformed her newfound technique of curves and angles and simplicity, but showed that a group of women dancers on stage could command it on their own without partners. Presented in three segments: "Hymn to the Virgin," "Crucifix," and "Hosannah," in which the dancers enter and depart in sacred silence. "The dancers stalk in dead silence, with long, reaching legs, the foot brought to the earth with heavy forcefulness, as though staking out territory; the steps stretch, claim, demand a weight of body, of personality, and of presence, like an invading army."[74] The choir of dancers circle around the Virgin figure throughout the dance, much like the ancient dancers of the past who performed their rituals to the Virgin Mary.

Martha, as the Virgin wore a white cotton dress[75] cut like that of a paper doll, with large, loose sleeves and seemingly without seams, her hair hanging loose down her back, straight as a horse's tail, Indian style...It culminates in the crowning of the heavenly blessed maiden while she sits on the ground, crouched against the spread knees of her attendant, leaning back as the woman suddenly fixes behind her head – nails, an aureole of spread fingers. It's a gesture rude and emphatic, implanting the instant splendor while stamping each foot. The rays seem to bloom from the attendant's groin; the sudden god-head is visceral.[76]

Primitive Mysteries was punctuated with total silence, and was a risk for Graham because audiences (even her die-hard fans) were used to musical accompaniment. The piece almost was not presented because Graham (as was her wont) was hysterical at rehearsal, screaming at the dancers: "You don't care. You don't want to be good. Get out of the theater. Get out of my sight. Go home. Go away."[77] She knew and feared that if the dance was not articulated with reverence and seriousness, it could have dissolved into caricature. Gertrude Schuss, one of the original dancers in the piece, described the rehearsals for *Primitive Mysteries.*

> I think in presenting us with *Primitive Mysteries*, Martha really gave us a marvelous quietness that permeated the whole group. Everyone felt it, this belief in oneness. And when I was near her, she had the mystic verity of a figure to be worshipped. When she put out her hand to bless, when she touched you, when she was performing, it was not Martha, it was the Other. Even though the extension of her fingers or the gentleness of her hands – and, you know, they were rarely gentle in ordinary life – a vibration took over her being; you saw it in her face, you felt it in her body.[78]

Graham had *become* the Virgin Mary, and that embodiment of her character was not only apparent to the audience members, but also to the dancers. What particular rites she used to transform herself into the Virgin Mary, I do not know, however, her entrance and dancing on stage was indicative of total possession: of the Virgin Mary, of the dance, and of the Divine energies that I believe flowed through her.

Her manifestation of the Divine in *Primitive Mysteries* was apparent to those who knew her and danced with her, and this theme is repeated over and over. "She [Graham] equated art with religion and she thought that anyone who did this was possessed a little bit by God."[79] Glen Tetley, a former Graham dancer remarked cryptically that he was sure that "she felt she was the Chosen One and she had been given by Divine grace this tremendous power which she had."[80] Even Martha knew she possessed that power, and in her notebooks she wrote: "That driving force of God that plunges through me is what I live for."[81] I believe that Graham's awareness of this mystical energy is the same energy that drives mystics to seek union with God. In a mystic's case it is through prayer; in Graham's case, it was through *her* prayer to God through the dance.

The Director

In 1933, Graham accepted an offer to direct "Six Miracle Plays" staged for the Stage Alliance of the Guild Theatre in New York, and although this was a unique opportunity for her to direct, she felt that "she had allowed [financial] desperation for leading her off her path."[82] It was the first time that she would be the director of dramatic material on the stage. The six segments of the play included: "Lamentation of the Virgin Mary," "The Madeleine," "The Miraculous Birth and The Midwives," " Lees Trios Marries," "La Naiveté," ending with "Lees Trios Marries." Graham danced the role of the Virgin Mary in the first, second, third and fifth plays. Horst was her ever-present musical director for this production. In an article about the pageant, one critic wrote: "It was the work of Ruth St. Denis which first turned her [Graham's] attention from dramatic to the dance…Miss Graham finds it fascinating to direct a dramatic production in which pageantry and miming play an important part as they do in Miracle plays. She deplores the departure of the Anglo-Saxon Theatre on which the Greek Theatre was built, feeling that this departure is

Martha Speaks

I danced at St. Mark's in the Bowery, a wonderful old church in the East Village set up in the form of an old meeting house. I was in front of the altar rail they had then. I wore a blue dress and I hovered over the crib, which represented the crib of the baby Jesus. The Bishop turned to one of his associates and said, "What is she doing?" And he slowly took off all of his insignia, one by one, the collar, the ring, and so on. All this I could see very clearly as I began my dance. Not exactly a strong confidence builder; it just got me mad. After he watched me dance for a while he put them back on. His disapproval of the dance seemed to have ended. He realized I was not going to create a scandal; it was safe to return to being the Bishop. I was all right, I guess. – BM, 141.

responsible for the colloquialism of American acting, depriving it of rhythm. She believes thoroughly in the synchronization of the arts."[83] Not only was her directorial expertise helpful to her career in later years, but Graham was always aware of the integration of dance with the other components of performance, although dance was the primary focus of her work.

Her directorial debut and performance as the Virgin Mary earned her both praise and criticism in various publications. One critic wrote, "As the Virgin, in four of the six plays, Miss Graham showed once how extraordinary she is as a mime. Her gestures, her widespread attitudes, and her haunting, almost carved expressions were alive with eloquence."[84] Mary Watkins, although not enthusiastic for the performance as a whole, was quick to single out Graham's performance.

> The Six Miracle Plays might as well have been called mystery plays or problem plays, the mystery being why they were given, and the problem to find the precise angle of approaching the subject. Miss Graham is the one figure which emerges triumphant. Had the production been frankly designated as a dance stylization based on medieval miracle-play tradition, no praise would have been too high. Miss Graham, herself, is in every fiber of her artistic nature, eminently equipped for such work, which is at once human and wooden, intimate and remote, spare and beautiful…Her style and her art, ceremonial, shorn of superfluities, angular, rigid, recollected and humble, relate her congenially to those elder artists who worked unwittingly, even as she now works in the supreme sophistication.[85]

Graham was in her forties, and coming into her own as an artist. Although the miracle plays did not garner as much praise as *Primitive Mysteries,* they gave her a theatrical calling card as a director and allowed her to hold the reins for the entire production. She knew she would have to include a more derivative style of dancing, but it was also a smart move for her, for as the director, she had control, experience, and a unique opportunity that would serve her well in the future.

The Graham Legacy

Martha Graham continued to create and perform for her entire life – at age ninety-seven, when she died, she was at work on an unfinished piece called *Goddess*. Although her company has endured more than their share of legal problems since her death, fighting court battles for the rights to perform her choreography, Graham's insights, intuitive sense, and most of all understanding of the body remain in all of her pieces. In 1933, John Martin wrote: "Her dancing is essentially religious in character, not that it deals in symbols of piety or moral preachments, but that it concerns itself with the forces of the universe."[86] Her acute knowledge of those forces is apparent in her choreographic legacy and is a potent vehicle for returning us as a public to participate and share in watching dance as a sacred and spiritual experience. Through her brilliant choreographic lens, the genius of Martha Graham will never die.

A Tribute
Martha Graham

Into the dark and into the light
The more you dance in the dark;
Dance your way to wisdom
And dance out with the spark.

We hardly knew but now we know,
The angular pattern of the puritan mind
And the puritan pattern the curious curve
Bends over to find.

Man's body is the music and the soul,
And where the dream imperfect, ugly or mean,
The tents of his hope are lifted
And even the tainted raised clean,

Remember us, remember us good
And dance, dance near, dance near.[87]

– Owen Dodson

While Graham's legacy continues specifically through the devoted members of the Martha Graham Dance Company, her words on the future of dance are a timeless gift to all dancers, and certainly applicable to our era.

My plea is that there are certain things I'd desperately like to see. I'd like to see all dancers, all of the companies highly geared, highly trained with a gift of something to say. I have a bitterness against only one thing – mediocrity. I feel that the standards must be held. The standards are held physically in the dance, but I think, choreographically, there is self-indulgence. And if the dance dies or falls, it will not be because of the audience; it will be a corruption from within – that the standards are not high enough, not demanding enough, and that what you see on the stage is not ravishing enough. You should be ravished by what you see; it should leave a mark on your life.[88]

May all of you be ravished in your lives.

"Mary Blessing the World."
Courtesy of photographer Scott Hess.

Endnotes

TITLE ABBREVIATIONS

AOG   Blackmer, Joan Dexter. *Acrobats of the Gods: Dance and Transformation*. Toronto: Inner City, 1989.

AUL   St. Denis, Ruth. *An Unfinished Life*. New York: Harper and Bros., 1939.

BM   Graham, Martha. *Blood Memory*. New York: Doubleday, 1991.

BWTF   Melle, Harro, *Bought We This Freedom*. New York: Richard Smith Inc, 1949.

CM   Heline, Corinne. *Color and Music in the New Age*. La Canada, Calif.: New Age, 1964.

CRS   Steiner, Rudolph. *Colour*. London: Rudolph Steiner Press, 1992.

CS   Portmann, Adolf. *Color Symbolism from the Eranos Yearbook, 1972*. Dallas: Spring, 1977.

CWMG   Tobias, Toby. From "A Conversation with Martha Graham," *Dance Magazine*, March, 1984.

DAG   Lawler, Lillian. *The Dance in Ancient Greece*. Middletown, Conn.: Wesleyan, 1964.

DD   Shelton, Suzanne. *Divine Dancer: A Biography of Ruth St. Denis*. New York: Doubleday, 1981.

DODD   Sherman, Jane. *The Drama of Denishawn Dance*. Middletown, Conn.: Wesleyan, 1979.

DMS   Charlton, Hilda. *Divine Mother Speaks*. Woodstock, N.Y.: Golden Quest, 1993.

DM   Roseman, Janet. *Dance Masters: Interview with Legends of Dance*. New York: Routlege, 2001.

DRJ   Sklar, Diedre. From "Felt knowledge and the Danzantes of Tortugas, New Mexico" in *Dance Research Journal*, Fall 1999.

GOG   Vignier, Rachel. *Gestures of Genius; Women, Dance and The Body*. Ontario: Mercury, 1994.

GR   Novick, Leah Rabbi. From "Encountering the Shechinah, The Jewish Goddess." *The Goddess Re-Awakening: The Feminine Principal Today*. Wheaton, Illinois: Quest, 1989.

HF   Wheeler, Marion. *Her Face: Images of the Virgin Mary in Art*. Cobb, Calif.: First Glance, 1998.

IAR   MacDougal, Allan Ross. *Isadora: A Revolutionary in Art and Love*. New York: Thomas Nelson, 1960.

ID   Terry, Walter. *Isadora Duncan: Her Life, Her Art, Her Legacy*. New York: Mead, 1963.

IDCF   Isadora Duncan Clipping Files. Courtesy of the Jerome Robbins Dance Collection, Dance Clipping Files, New York City Library of Performing Arts.

IP   Blair, Fredericka. *Isadora: Portrait of the Artist As A Woman*. New York: McGraw Hill, 1986.

IRSD   Ubell, Earl. "Interview with Ruth St. Denis." (Tape), 1964. Isadora Duncan Files, Courtesy of Jerome Robbins Dance Collection, Dance Clipping Files, New York City Library of Performing Arts.

IS   Duncan, Isadora. *Isadora Speaks*. San Francisco: City Lights, 1981.

ITM   Schlundt, Christina. From "Into the Mystic With Miss Ruth." In *Dance Perspectives*, 46, Summer, 1971.

JKJ   Shamdasani, Sonu. C.J. Jung: *The Psychology of Kundalini Yoga*. Princeton: Bollingen, 1996.

KE   Yuasa, Yasuo. *The Body, Self-Cultivation and Ki-Energy*. Alba, New York: SUNY, 1993.

LH   Soares, Janet Mansfield. *Louis Horst: Musician in a Dancer's World*. London: Duke, 1992.

LL   St. Denis, Ruth. *Lotus Light: Poems by Ruth St. Denis*. New York: Houghton-Mifflin, © 1932, renewed 1960 by Ruth St. Denis.

LOM   Jameson, Mrs. *Legends of the Madonna As Represented in the Fine Arts*. Detroit: Omnigraphics, 1990.

LUA   Duncan, Dore, et al. *Life Unto Art: Isadora Duncan and Her World*. New York: Norton, 1993.

MAR   DeMille, Agnes. *Martha*. New York: Vintage, 1991.

MDP   Graham, Martha. "A Modern Dancer's Primer for Action," in: Selma Jean Cohen, Ed. *Dance as Theatre Art: Source Readings in Dance History from 1581 to the present*. Princeton, N.J.: Princeton University Press, 1974, second edition.

ML   Duncan, Isadora. *My Life*. New York: Liveright, 1927.

MGAB   McDonagh, Don. *Martha Graham: A Biography*. New York: Preager, 1973.

MG   DeMille, Agnes. "Martha Graham." From *The Atlantic*. Date unknown.

MGDR   Tracy, Robert. *Goddess: Martha Graham Dancers Remember*. New York: Limelight, 1996.

MGT   Horosko, Miriam. *Martha Graham: The Evolution of Her Dance Theory and Training*. New York: a capella, 1991.

MRLL   Terry, Walter. *Miss Ruth: The More Living Life of Ruth St. Denis*. New York: Dodd Mead, 1969.

NEW   Ashton, Dore. *Noguchi East and West*. Berkeley: University of California, 1992.

NYCB   Chujoy, Anatole. *The New York City Ballet*. New York: Knopf, 1953.

NYMG Martha Graham Clipping Files, Courtesy of Jerome Robbins Dance Collection, Dance Clipping Files, New York City Library of Performing Arts.

NYMG-TFA Adolphe, Roberts, W. "The Fervid Art of Martha Graham," August 1928. Courtesy of Jerome Robbins Dance Collection, Dance Clipping Files, New York City Library of Performing Arts

PAM Lamb, Susan. *Pueblo and Mission*. Flagstaff, Arizona: Northland, 1997.

PMC Whitehead, Nicholas. *Patterns in Magical Christianity*. Albuquerque, New Mexico: Sun Chalice, 1996.

POTD Dickson, Edward. *Poems of the Dance. New York*: Alfred A. Knopf, 1921.

PTP Pagan, Isabelle M. *From Pioneer to Poet*. London: Theosophical Publishing, 1930.

RDCC Bachman, Louis E. *Religious Dances*. London: George Allen and Unwin, 1952.

RMGD King, Francis. *Ritual Magic of the Golden Dawn*. Rochester, Vermont: Destiny, 1987.

RSD Ruth St. Denis Files, Courtesy of Jerome Robbins Dance Collection, Dance Clipping Files, New York City Library of Performing Arts.

SWSD Stewart, Iris. *Sacred Woman, Sacred Dance*. Rochester, Vermont: Inner Traditions, 2000.

TAF Schmidt-Brabant, Manfred. *The Archtypal Feminine*. London: Temple Lodge, 1998.

TAOD Duncan, Isadora. *The Art of the Dance*. New York: Theatre Arts, 1969.

TCH Sharamon, Shalila. *The Chakra Handbook*. Wilmot, Wisc.: Limelight, 1996.

TGM Kingsley, David. *The Goddesses' Mirror*. New York: SUNY, 1989.

TNOMG Ross, Nancy Wilson. *The Notebooks of Martha Graham*. New York: Harcourt, Brace, Jovanovitch, 1973.

TPSC Loney, Glenn. *Unsung Genius*. New York: Franklin Watts, 1984.

TRI Seroff, Victor. *The Real Isadora*. New York: Dial, 1963.

TRY Schneider, Ilya Ulyich. *Isadora Duncan: The Russian Years*. New York: Harcourt, Brace, World, 1968.

TSI Regnier, Kathleen. *The Spiritual Image In Modern Art*. London: Quest, 1987.

TVMC Ashe, Geoffrey. *The Virgin*. London: Arkana, 1976.

YI Steegmuller, Francis. *Yours Isadora*. New York: Random House, 1974.

UL St. Denis, Ruth. *Ruth St. Denis*. New York: Harper and Brothers, 1939.

WCD Miller, Kamae. *Wisdom Comes Dancing*. Seattle, Wash.: Peaceworks, 1997.

WSD Kendall, Elizabeth. *Where She Danced*. New York: Knopf, 1979.

Introduction

1 Franklin Rosemont, (ed.) *Isadora Speaks* (San Francisco: City Lights, 1981), 24. Hereafter, **IS**.

2 Joan Dexter Blackmer, *Acrobats of the Gods: Dance and Transformation* (Toronto: Inner City. 1989), 23-24. Hereafter, **AOG**.

3 Walter Sorrell, "Sacred Dance Revisited," *Dance Magazine*, June 1962, 17.

4 Rachel Vignier, *Gestures of Genius, Women, Dance, and The Body* (Ontario: Mercury. 1994), 42. Hereafter, **GOG**.

5   Ruth St. Denis, *An Unfinished Life* (New York: Harper &Brothers, 1939), 71. Hereafter, **AUL**.

6   Iris Stewart, *Sacred Woman, Sacred Dance* (Rochester, Vermont: Inner Traditions, 2001), 7. Hereafter **SWSD**.

7   Martha Graham, *The Notebooks of Martha Graham* (New York: Harcourt, Brace, Jovanovitch, 1973), 25. Hereafter, **TNOMG**.

8   Robin Robertson. "Untitled." *Gnosis*, Fall 1998, 40.

9   Neil Douglas-Klotz, "Ruth St. Denis: Sacred Dance Explorations in America," in *Dance as Religious Studies*. Ed. Doug Adams. (New York: Crossroad, 1993), 111.

10   Ruth St. Denis, *Lotus Light* (Boston: Houghton Mifflin, 1932), 88.

11   This is often referred to as "tactile clairvoyance" according to Shalia Sharamon and Bodo J. Baginski, authors of *The Chakra Handbook* (Wilmot, Wisc.: Lotus Light, 1991), 56.

12   Sonu Shamdasani, (ed.), *C.J. Jung: The Psychology of Kundalini Yoga.* (Princeton: Bollingen XCIX, 1996). Hereafter, **JKJ**.

13   Isadora Duncan, *The Art of the Dance.* (New York: Theatre Arts Books, 1969), 101.

Chapter 1

1   Mayer Gruber, "Ten Dance-Derived Expressions in the Hebrew Bible," *from Dance as Religious Studies* (New York: Crossroad, 1993), 48.

2   Louis E. Backman, *Religious Dances in the Christian Church and in Popular Medicine* (London: George Allen and Unwin, 1952), 70.

3   Ibid., 70. Hereafter, **RDCC.**

4   Janet Lynn Roseman, *Dance Masters: Interviews with Legends of Dance* (New York: Routledge, 2001).

5   Lillian Lawler, *The Dance in Ancient Greece.*(Middletown, Conn.: Wesleyan, 1964), 31-33.

6   Ibid., 31-33. Hereafter, **DAG**.

7   **RDCC**, 36.

8   Layne Redmond, *When the Drummers Were Men: A Spiritual History of Rhythm* (New York: Three Rivers, 1997), 120.

9   **RDCC**, 29.

10   Susanne F. Fincher, *Creating Mandalas For Insight, Healing, and Self-Expression* (Boston: Shambhala, 1991), 10.

11   **RDCC**, 200.

12   Author unknown, from http://hdlighthouse.org/abouthd/hd-facts/updates/0030dancing.shtml.

13   **SWSD**, 313.

14   **SWSD**, 39.

15   Ed. Kamae Miller, *Wisdom Comes Dancing: Selected Writings of Ruth St. Denis on Dance, Spirituality and the Body* (Seattle: Peaceworks, 1997), 206.

16 Ibid., 50. Hereafter, **WCD**.

17 Marion Woodman, "Human Potential Through Dance," in *Conscious Femininity* (Toronto: Inner City, 1993), 152.

18 Stuart Hodes, from "Blood Memory," in *Ballet Review*, Fall 1991, 4.

19 St. Symeon the New Theologian, quoted in: Cynthia Bourgeault, *Mystical Hope: Trusting in the Mercy of God.* (Boston: Cowley Publications, 2001), xi-xii.

20 **WCD**, 75.

21 Jonathan Cott, "Two Talks with George Balanchine" in *Portrait of Mr. B.* (New York: Viking, 1984), 133.

22 Isadora Duncan, *The Art of the Dance* (San Francisco: City Lights, 1981) 49. Hereafter, **TAOD**.

23 St. Theresa Àvila, quoted in "Sudden Rapture," *Parabola*, Summer 1998, No.2, 66. See *The Interior Castle* for further study.

24 **GOG**, 178.

25 Martha Graham, *Blood Memory* (New York: Doubleday, 1991), 68.

26 Ibid., 117-118. Hereafter, **BM**.

27 Dorothy Bird, *Bird's Eye View: Dancing with Martha Graham and On Broadway* (Pittsburgh: University of Pittsburgh, 1997), 116.

28 **AUL**, 86-87

29 **GOG**, 22.

30 **GOG**, 23.

31 Manfred Schmidt-Brabant, *The Archetypal Feminine* (London: Temple Lodge, 1998), 29.

32 Mark Garrison, In "The Nature of Maenadism in Ancient Greece." From www:http//www/trinity/edu/mgarrison/Vases/VaseProjects/WP/maenad-nature.html.

33 Ibid., 3.

34 **DAG,** 76.

35 Manfred Schmidt-Brabant, 12.

36 **TAOD**, 33.

37 Geoffrey Ashe, *The Virgin: Mary's Cult and the Re-Emergence of the Goddess* (London: Arkana, 1976), 150.

38 Ibid., 150. Hereafter, **TVMC**.

39 Mrs. Jameson, *Legends of the Madonna As Represented in the Fine Arts* (2nd ed. Detroit: Omigraphics, 1990), 20.

40 **SWSD**, 69.

41 Maurice Hamington, *Hail Mary? The Struggle for Ultimate Womanhood in Catholicism* (New York: Routledge, 1995), 18.

42 David Kinsley, *The Goddesses' Mirror: Visions of the Divine from East to West* (New York: State University of New York, 1989), 222.

43 Ibid., 222. Hereafter, **TGM**.

44 **SWSD**, 37.

45 Marion Wheeler, *Her Face: Images of the Virgin Mary in Art* (Cobb, California: First Glance, 1998), 15. Hereafter, **HF**.

46 **SWSD**, 37.

47 **HF**, 141.

48 Anneli S. Rufus and Kristan Lawson, *Goddess Sites: Europe* (New York: Harper, 1991), 14.

49 **RSD**, 45.

50 **RSD**, 45.

51 **RSD**, 78

52 **RSD**, 37.

53 Deirdre Sklar, "Felt Knowledge and Danzantes of Tortugas, New Mexico," in *Dance Research Journal*, Fall 1999, 17.

54 Ibid., 27.

Chapter 2

1   Fredricka Blair, *Isadora: Portrait of the Artist as a Woman* (New York: McGraw Hill, 1986), 6. Isadora was baptized several month later and the date given for the birth year was 1877. However, her older brother Augustin claimed she was born in 1878. Raymond, another brother, insisted that the date was 1877, which aligns with baptismal records. Hereafter referred to as **IP**.

2   Isabelle M. Pagan, *From Pioneer to Poet: An Expansion of the Signs of the Zodiac Analyzed* (London: Theosophical Publishing, 1930), 44. Hereafter referred to as **PTP**.

3   What the reference is to "its power," I can only surmise as the power of divinity or Spirit coursing through her veins.

4   **IP**, 26.

5   Isadora Duncan, *My Life* (New York: Horace Liveright, 1927), 18. Hereafter, **ML**.

6   Ibid., 21.

7   **TAOD**, 79.

8   **ML**, 23.

9   Ibid., 80.

10 Erté, *Erté: Things I Remember* (New York: Quadrangle, 1975), 33. In his book, he offers an amusing story about the bewitching charisma that Duncan had. "In real life she was not beautiful, but her vibrant personality created its own legend. Once she asked Georgette Leblanc, then married to Maurice Maeterlinck, if she could 'borrow' her husband for a few days. The child conceived in this temporary union, she explained would be the most perfect human being imaginable. It would inherit her own beauty and Maeterlinck's genius."33. Maeterlinck was a poet known for his spiritual writings, which would explain Duncan's attraction to him.

11 **ML**, 90.

12 Robert Henri, *The Art Spirit* (New York: Harper and Row, 1958), 245.

13 Walter Terry, *Isadora Duncan: Her Life, Her Art, Her Legacy* (New York: Dodd Mead,1963), 87. Hereafter referred to as **ID**.

14 **IS**, 50.

15 Wassily Kandinsky, *Concerning the Spiritual in Art* (M.T.H. Sadler, Translator) (New York: Dover, 1977) Dover edition, 50-51. The first edition was titled *On the Spiritual in Art and Painting in Particular.*

16 The translator's note on this page indicates that he believes "Duncan is not perhaps perfectly chosen." He argues that Duncan was only concerned with attaining "beauty," but what he doesn't understand is that Duncan's idea of beauty was not only external in nature, but produced from the "inner spirit."

17 **GOG**, 47.

18 Kenneth C. Lindsay, Peter Vergo, *Kandinsky: Complete Writings on Art* (New York: DeCapo, 1994) 202, 205.

19 Dore Duncan, et. al. *Life Unto Art: Isadora Duncan and Her World* (New York: Norton, 1993), 49. Hereafter, **LUA**.

20 **GOG**, 48.

21 Ibid., 18.

22 Francis Steegmuller (Ed.) *"Your Isadora": The Love Story of Isadora Duncan and Gordon Craig Told Through their Letters and Diaries Never Before Published* (New York; Random House, 1974), 212. Hereafter referred to as **YI**.

23 Ibid., 214.

24 William James, *The Varieties of Religious Experience* (London: Longmans, Green and Co., 1935), 380.

25 **ML**, 213.

26 Wassily Kandinsky's groundbreaking work "Concerning the Spiritual in Art" was published in English in 1912 in English. Duncan was a voracious reader, and it is possible she read this work.

27 Nadia Choucha, *Surrealism & the Occult; Shamanism, Magic, Alchemy, and the Birth of an Artistic Movement* (Rochester, Vermont: Destiny, 1992), 21.

28 Kathleen Regnier, *The Spiritual Image in Modern Art* (London: Quest, 1987), 41. Hereafter, **TSI**.

29 Thomas Buser, "Gauguin's Religion," In **TSI**, 40.

30 **ML**, 130.

31 Melinda Boyd Parsons, "Mysticism in London: The 'Golden Dawn' Synaesthesia, and 'Psychic-Automatism' in the Art of Pamela Colman Smith," 40-41. In **TSI**.

32 However, Duncan would marry in her lifetime.

33 **TAOD**, 73.

34 Ibid., 66-67.

35 **ML**, 157.

36 Meditation, which is an integral component for spiritual practice, posed challenges for Duncan and in a brief letter to lover, Gordon Craig, she explained: "Can you sit truly still on a Lily Pad and meditate? I tried it – it is dreadful and difficult – I've no doubt it is an art like being a great musician." **TAOD**, 139.

37 **TSI**, 80.

38 Ibid., 80-81.

39 **TAOD**, 123-124.

40 **YI**, 79.

41 Adolf Portmann, et. al. *Color Symbolism* (Eranos Series 1, Dallas: Spring, 1977), 95. Hereafter referred to as **CS**.

42 Maria Schindler, "The Allegorical Symbolical and Mystical Use of Colour: Extracts from a Theory of Colours," In *Pure Colour, Part 1. Goethe's Theory of Colour Applied* (London: New Cultures, 1946), 86-87.

43 **CS**, 113.

44 S.J. Ousleley, *Colour Meditations* (London: L.N. Fowler & Co., 1949), 17.

45 **ML**, 96-97.

46 Kathleen Alexander-Berghorn, "Isis: The Goddess as Healer" In *The Goddess Re-Awakening*, Ed. Shirley Nicholson, (Wheaton, Illinois: Quest, 1989), 93. Hereafter **TG**.

47 Hilda Charlton, *Divine Mother Speaks* (Woodstock, N.Y.: Golden Quest, 1993) 21. Hereafter, **DM**.

48 Ibid. 18.

49 **TAOD**, 55.

50 Ibid., 56.

51 **TGM**, 95. On pg. 95, Marion Weinstein suggested that the initiates of the mysteries of Isis emulated the Goddess by learning to work with words of power, which she believed were affirmation techniques used for healing and self-transformation. No doubt Duncan was very well versed in goddess worship and history.

52 **IP**, 398. Garcia Marsellac sang *Ave Maria* to the 4000 people who attended Isadora's funeral at the famous Pére Lachaise cemetery.

53 Mary Daly, *Beyond God the Father: Toward A Philosophy of Woman's Liberation* (Boston: Beacon Press, 1977), 78-80.

54 Allan Ross Macdougal, *Isadora: A Revolutionary in Art and Love* (New York: Thomas Nelson, 1960), 173-174.

55 Ibid. 173.

56 **YI,** 187.

57 Ilya Ulyich Schneider, *Isadora Duncan; The Russian Years* (New York: Harcourt, Brace & World, 1968), 51. Hereafter referred to as **TRY**.

58 Corinne Heline, *Color and Music in The New Age* (La Canada, California: New Age, 1964), 111-112. Hereafter referred to as **CM**.

59   Interestingly, "ave" is also the reverse of "eve" or perhaps Eve. According to writers Manfred Schmidt-Brabant and Virginia Sease in their book *The Archetypal Feminine: in the Mystery Stream of Humanity; Towards a New Culture of the Family* (London: Temple, 1999), 17, Mary is also considered the second Eve. Hereafter referred to as **TAF**.

60   Courtesy of the Jerome Robbins Dance Collection, Dance Clipping Files, New York City Library of Performing Arts. Hereafter referred to as **IDCF**. Mary Fanton Roberts, "Isadora the Dancer." *The Denishawn Magazine.* (date unknown) 13.

61   **ML**, 263.

62   **IDCF**, untitled document.

63   **LUA**, 119. Although Duncan became pregnant again by a young Italian sculptor (whom she never named), the baby boy died immediately after he was born.

64   **IDCF**, untitled document.

65   **ML**, 278.

66   Ibid., 314-315.

67   Ibid., 275.

68   In Sisley Huddleston's book, *Paris Salons, Cafes, Studios: Being Social Artistic and Literary Memories* (Philadelphia: Lippincott, 1928), 193, there is an account that on the day of the children's burial, Duncan performed *Chopin's Marche Funebre* played for her by the Orchestre Colonne, much to the chagrin of the countrymen and women of Paris. "I could not understand that she should express such emotions through the medium of the dance." This conflicts with other reports in many books on Duncan. Mary Fanton Roberts, a friend wrote in her essay, "Isadora – The Dancer," (*The Denishawn Magazine*), "She did not dance at all, although every day she used to watch her school dancing in the long blue salon."

69   **LUA**, 121.

70   **ML**, 297.

71   **ML**, 296.

72   **IP**, 246-247.

73   **TRY**, 49.

74   Ibid., 50-51.

75   Collier's article was published in *Survey* on June 3, 1916, 251.

76   **IP**, 243.

77   Ibid., 243.

78   Ibid., 243.

79   Irma Duncan, *Duncan Dancer* (Middletown, Conn.: Wesleyan, 1966), 216.

80   Ibid., 216.

81   **IDCF**, untitled document, 1961.

82   **IDCF**, Ernest Haskell, "The Matinee Girl Column," *The New York Dramatic Mirror*, May 9, 1903.

83   Ibid. 216.

84 **IDCF**, untitled document.

85 **TRI**, 156.

86 **ID**, 66.

87 Ibid., 138.

88 Victor Seroff, *The Real Isadora* (New York: Dial), 286. Hereafter, **TRI**.

89 Ibid., 421.

90 Ibid., 422.

91 **ID**, 110-111.

92 Ibid., 110-111.

93 Ibid., 110-111.

94 **TRI**, 422.

95 Ibid., 425.

96 This interview is contained in my book: *Dance Masters: Interviews with Legends of Dance* (New York: Routledge, 2001), 92.

97 Anatole Chujoy, *The New York City Ballet* (New York: Alfred A. Knopf, 1953), 64.

98 Lincoln Kirstein, *Lincoln Kirstein's Thirty Years: The New York City Ballet* (New York: Knopf, 1978), 37.

99 Bernard Taper, *Balanchine: A Biography* (Berkeley: University of California, 1984), 59.

100 **ID**, 57.

101 From the film, *Isadora Duncan: Technique and Repertory Dance.* Dance Horizons, 1995.

102 Ibid.

103 Lois Palken Rudnick, *Mabel Dodge Luhan: New Woman, New Worlds* (Albuquerque: University of New Mexico,1984) 121.

104 Joan Acocella, and Lynn Garafola, (Eds.) *Andre Levinson on Dance: Writings from Paris in the Twenties* (Hanover, New Hampshire: Wesleyan, 1991), 13.

105 **ID**, 155.

106 Nicholas Whitehead, *Patterns in Magical Christianity* (Albuquerque, New Mexico: Sun Chalice, 1996), 58. Hereafter, **PMC**.

107 Francis King, *Ritual Magic of the Golden Dawn* (Rochester, Vermont: Destiny, 1987), 144. Hereafter **RMGD**.

108 **TAOD**, 51-52.

109 **RMGD**, 211.

110 Karla McLaren, *Your Aura and Your Chakras; The Owner's Manual* (York Beach, Maine: Weiser, 1998), 178.

111 **TAOD**, 138.

112 Metaphysical philosophers Gurdjieff and Ouspensky used this term "the magnetic center." Did Duncan study their books and teachings? Most probably, although I have not uncovered a direct validation in my research.

113 **ML**, 75-76.

114 Ibid., 112.

115 Ibid., 350.

116 Peter Kurth, *Isaadora: A Sensational Life* (New York: Little, Brown and Co., 2001), 383.

117 **YI**, 359-361.

Chapter 3

1 **PTP**, 145.

2 She dropped the extra "n" when her name changed to Ruth St. Denis.

3 Albert Goldberg, from *Los Angeles Times*, February 2, 1964. "Ruth St. Denis, Prophet of Dance: 85, Still Kicking." Courtesy of Jerome Robbins Dance Collection, Dance Clipping Files, New York City Library of Performing Arts. Hereafter, **RSD**.

4 **AUL**, 6.

5 Ibid., 2.

6 Ibid., 7.

7 Ibid., 5.

8 From an article entitled, "The Dance as Life Experience," 1925. *Denishawn Magazine*. Pg. 1-3. Vol. 1. No. 1. Courtesy of the Jerome Robbins Dance Collection, Dance Clipping Files, New York City Library of Performing Arts.

9 Ruth would later be affectionately called "Miss Ruth" by her students, and even by the press.

10 Jane Sherman, *The Drama of Denishawn Dance* (Middletown, Conn.: Wesleyan, 1979), 3. Hereafter referred to as **DODD**. Evidently, Belasco was romantically interested in St. Denis who had rebuffed his advances while she maintained a "friendship" with noted architect Stanford White. When the subject of marriage came up during a party, Belasco made the comment. According to St. Denis in her autobiography, *An Unfinished Life*, 42: "This was a little dig at my lack of emotional response to him."

11 From private correspondence with Regina Sara Ryan, October, 2003. Ryan added that, "The universe is coded, and such a name taken at such an early age was probably the result of a soul connection to something much deeper than either she or her mother had any idea about."

12 **AUL**, 68.

13 Andrew M. Greeley, *Ecstasy: A Way of Knowing* (Englewood Cliffs, New Jersey: Prentice Hall,1974), 4.

14 **RSD**. Her longtime partner at Denishawn, the school she created with Ted Shawn, would write the book, *Ruth St. Denis: Pioneer and Prophet*, about her.

15 Abraham J. Heschel, *The Prophets: An Introduction*. Vol. I. (New York: Harper Collins, 1962), 9.

16 Miller's excellent book, *Wisdom Comes Dancing: Selected Writings on Ruth St. Denis on Dance, Spirituality and the Body* (Seattle; Peaceworks, 1997) is an important resource on St. Denis. As previously mentioned **WCD**.

17 Neil Douglas-Klotz, Ed., In *Sufi Vision and Initiation; Meetings with Remarkable Beings.* (San Francisco: Sufi Islamia/Prohphecy Publications, 1986), 320.

18 **RSD**

19 **CM**, 33.

20 Even my former dance teacher mistakenly told me that St. Denis never traveled to the Orient, never researched her dances, and simply made them up. Of course she made them up, but there are a number of sources outside of her own journals that specify that she always did a great deal of research, and her tours to the Orient are documented.

21 Evelyn Underhill, *Practical Mysticism* (Columbus, Ohio: Ariel, 1986), 43, 48. Note that the first edition of this book was released in 1914, when St. Denis, a great devourer of all things mystical, must have found it. When you consider that St. Denis grew up on a farm and was not educated in the traditional sense, her genius is even more apparent in her writings *and* her choreographic works.

22 Elizabeth Kendall, *Where She Danced* (New York: Knopf, 1979), 50. Hereafter referred to as **WSD**. Although the story of Radha and Krishna depicts Radha as a mortal, she becomes more than woman in St. Denis's choreography. "To become Radha she garbed herself in a gauze skirt with a gilt rim; she covered her midriff bodice with dimestore brooches and decapitated hatpins, she put two jeweled circles in her hair at the nape of her neck, and stained her body brown. She even tried a version of a nose-ring."

23 According to Ted Shawn, this solo did not last very long because of St. Denis's problems with the costume. "Ruth was always a mistress of multiple draperies, but this time she went too far and the costume mastered her! She tried to be not only the goddess of the Hawaiian volcano, but the whole volcano too!" In Walter Terry, *Miss Ruth: The More Living Life of Ruth St. Denis* (New York: Dodd Mead, 1969), 151. Hereafter referred to as **MRLL**.

24 Earl Ubell, *Interview with Ruth St. Denis.* (Tape), 1964. Courtesy of the Jerome Robbins Dance Collection, Dance Clipping Files, New York City Library of Performing Arts. Hereafter referred to as **IRSD**.

25 **AUL**, 52.

26 Ibid., 3.

27 Ibid., 54. She even asked her friend to retrieve the poster of Isis from the drugstore so she could pin it on her wall.

28 Suzanne Shelton, *Divine Dancer: A Biography of Ruth St. Denis* (New York: Doubleday, 1981), 114. Hereafter referred to as **DD**.

29 **IRSD**. St. Denis had many rabbis as her friends and valuable resources for her work, and she frequently mentions them in her autobiography.

30 **AUL**, 206.

31 Ruth St. Denis, "An Interpretation of the Various Religious Symbols Used by the Rhythmic Choir in Angels of the Liturgy," **RSD**, courtesy of the Jerome Robbins Dance Collection, Dance Clipping Files, New York City Library of Performing Arts.

32 **DODD**, 2.

33 Christina L. Schlundt, "Into the Mystic with Miss Ruth," *Dance Perspectives*, 46, Summer, 1971, 9. Hereafter referred to as **ITM**.

34 **DD**, 102.

35 **ITM**, 6.

36 Ibid., 6.

37 **WCD**, 86.

38 **DD**, 13. St. Denis would later study with Genevieve Stebbins, who expanded Delsarte's theories, integrating yoga, gymnastics, Buddhism, and oriental dances, all techniques and themes that would appear in St. Denis's dances in the future.

39 **WCD**, 31. Even though she studied the Delsarte system in great detail, and integrated it with her training for dancers at her dance center Denishawn, St. Denis would also add her own metaphysical and mystical ideas to the education of her dancers.

40 **AUL**, 119.

41 Shawn would leave to create his own success with the birth of Jacob's Pillow and his famous group of men dancers. His influence and relationship with St. Denis is most interesting historically and psychologically.

42 **AUL**, 247.

43 **AUL**, 254. Although St. Denis was financially highly-success in her lifetime, she ended her life with a very small monthly income provided for her from Shawn and St. Denis's brother, along with her fees for lecture tours.

44 Ibid., 253. St. Denis was well aware of the mechanical life that so many people were imprisoned within and this was just one of her visionary solutions to the problem, a problem that echoed Duncan's idea for schools across the world to educate children. However, in St. Denis's case, she was referring to an opportunity to bring dance to people of all races and ages.

45 According to Rob Baker's article "Hearing the Sound of Color," the *Gesamtkunstwerk* that artists Wassily Kandinsky and Thomas de Hartmann wanted to create "existed in direct connection to a *weltanschauung* – a total view of the universe. Not art for art's sake, but art at the service of higher meaning, both emotional and spiritual." Rob Baker, "Hearing the Sounds of Color," *Parabola*, Vol. VII, No.2, Spring, 1982, 92.

46 St. Denis has her dates confused because Duncan died in 1927. She gave this interview when she was in her eighties, so she no doubt couldn't remember the exact dates.

47 **IRSD**.

48 **AUL**, 57.

49 **ML**, 76.

50 **IS**, 54.

51 **LUA**, 29.

52 **RSD**. J.J. Dominique, "Dance: Tribute to Miss Ruth," *Springfield Herald*, 24, July 1969. Courtesy of the Jerome Robbins Dance Collection, Dance Clipping Files, New York City Library of Performing Arts.

53 Richard Edgar, Lovstron, "On Thomas Wilfred." https://www.gis.net/~scatt/clavilux/html.

54 **MRLL**, 192.

55 Ibid., 194.

56 No doubt Duncan would have continued to dance into her old age if she hadn't been killed at mid-life.

57 **RSD**. Walter Terry, From "A Rust-Free Body on Flying Carpet," date unknown. Courtesy of the Jerome Robbins Dance Collection, Dance Clipping Files, New York City Library of Performing Arts.

58 Carmen Kagal, "Indian Interlude in Modern Dance," *Span,* March 1966, 34.

59 **UL**, 156.

60 Ibid., 336.

61 **RSD**, untitled document.

62 **AUL**, 338-339.

63 **RSD**. It is quite telling that St. Denis was successful in offering her dances to a variety of Christian churches, not only one sect of Christianity. When I was researching her history, I went to Riverside Church in New York, but in their vast archive they did not possess any files or photos, or any information about St. Denis's many performances there.

64 **RSD**, from the Associated Press, Feb. 2, 1935.

65 **RSD**, untitled document.

66 **RSD**, untitled document.

67 From *The Denishawn Magazine*, Vol. I. no.1 pg. 1-2. Courtesy of the Jerome Robbins Dance Collection, Dance Clipping Files, New York City Library of Performing Arts

68 **IRSD**.

69 Her mystical experiences are again trivialized in the book, *Where She Danced*, by author, Elizabeth Kendall who writes, "Ruth thought she felt spiritual ecstasy." I don't think that Kendall can judge what St. Denis experienced, nor can anyone else, and to do so is impertinent. 48.

70 Ibid.

71 Walter Terry, *The Religious Dance*, **RSD**, 120. Courtesy of the Jerome Robbins Dance Collection, Dance Clipping Files, New York City Library of Performing Arts

72 Ibid.,121.

73 Glenn Loney, *Unsung Genius: The Passion of Dancer-Choreographer Jack Cole* (New York: Franklin Watts, 1984), 351. Whether or not Cole contributed monetarily to her vision is not clear from this source and I have been unable to document any additional sources that show that he contributed to her temple.

74 **WCD**, 131-132.

75 Ibid., 118.

76 Shakina Reinhertz, *Women Called to the Path of Rumi: The Way of the Whirling Dervish* (Prescott, Arizona: Hohm Press, 2001), 9.

77 Ibid., 10.

78 Talat Sait Halman and Metin And, *Mevlana Celaleddin Rumi and the Whirling Dervishes.* (Istanbul: Dost Publications, 1983), 63.

79 **AUL**, 375.

80 Also called "The Blue Madonna of St. Mark's."

81 Phone conversation with Karoun Tootikian in 1999. She died in 2000.

82 **AUL**, 241.

83 Stuart Smithers, "Bodies of Sleep, Garments of Skins," *Parabola,* Vol. XIX, No.3, Fall 1994, 7.

84 **AUL**, notes on dancing on 242.

85 **RSD**, from "Arts Are Chalices Holding Wine of God, Says St. Denis," 19, August 1952.

86 *The Gold Madonna,* soloist Deborah Zall. Courtesy of the Jerome Robbins Dance Collection, Dance Clipping Files, Special Collections. New York City Library of Performing Arts Library, Dance Special Collections, MGZIC9-5592.

87 St. Denis does not identify the original composer but describes it as "intricate voices in orchestra."

88 **DD**, 241. Turquoise was the color traditionally associated with the Madonna.

89 Ibid., 242.

90 When St. Denis created the *White Madonna* and the *Gold Madonna* she chose to alternate the use of white costumes with gold, however, the evolution of this dance is relevant. During her meetings at Denishawn House (then established in New York), she invited her friend Das Gupta of the Fellowships of Faith to observe a performance. The last ritual was to Mary, in which she depicted the *White Madonna.* "The girls performed a lovely candle plastique and then, with almost the gay reverence of childhood, brought, like the Tumbler of Our Lady, their individual offerings of youth and dancing." The meetings were so successful that they attracted audiences in great numbers and only stopped when St. Denis encountered "clouds of debt and other inharmonies." She also claims that until she performed *Gold Madonna* at Saint Mark's-in-the-Bowry in New York, she never presented this "temple service outside the walls of Denishawn." However, the newspaper articles list the piece as *Masque of Mary* with its premiere at the Riverside Church in New York. In addition to St. Denis's dancing to the Madonna, her organist, Mr. Goldworthy, arranged for one of her praise poems to be sung by the church choir, which pleased her greatly.

Although, no documentation exists that validates which praise poem she may have delivered during the *Masque of Mary* performance, St. Denis's poem "The Great Circle" is a tribute to her devotion.

91 Ibid., 242.

92 **RSD**. Courtesy of the Jerome Robbins Dance Collection, Dance Clipping Files, New York City Library of Performing Arts. From "Ruth St. Denis Seminar." Ruth would not

only present seminars on religion and dance, but also was the director of the Religious Arts Program at Adelphi College.

93 **RSD**. Courtesy of the Jerome Robbins Dance Collection, Dance Clipping Files, New York City Library of Performing Arts, *New York Times*, 30, December, 1934.

94 **RSD**. From "Ruth St. Denis Presents Temple Service Recital: offers Christian Ritual Dances at Chamber Music Hall," *Herald Tribune*, 8, December, 1941.

95 **RSD**. 13, August, 1942. Writer and paper not attributed.

96 Constantine, "Ruth St. Denis and the Divine Dance," *Dance*, 1948.

97 **RSD**, untitled document.

98 "Her yoke is a golden ornament, and her bonds are a cord of blue. You will wear her like a glorious robe, you will put her on like a crown of gladness." From "A Glorious Robe," Kathleen Norris, *Parabola*, Fall 1994, Vol. XIX, No. 3, 45.

99 **RSD**, Courtesy of the Jerome Robbins Dance Collection, Dance Clipping Files, New York City Library of Performing Arts. Wayne C. Smith, "Jacob's Pillow Annual Dance Season Opens," *The Springfield Union*, 1, July 1, 1959.

100 Gerda Lerner, *The Creation of Feminist Consciousness: From the Middle Ages to Eighteen-Seventy* (London: Oxford, 1993), 103.

101 **AUL**, 382.

102 **AUL**, 377-378.

103 Peter A. Kwasniewski, "Wise and Foolish Virgins," *Parabola*, Summer 1998, Vol. XXIII, No. 22, 23.

104 William James, *The Varieties of Religious Experience* (London: Longmans, Green & Co, 1935), 399.

105 **AUL**, 379.

106 **RSD**. Martha Graham, "Ruth St. Denis – 1878-1968."

Chapter 4

1 Graham suffered from alcoholism in the later years of her life.

2 **PTP**, 21-32.

3 Walter Terry, "Sex and Martha Graham," Courtesy of The Jerome Robbins Dance Collection, Dance Clipping Files, New York City Performing Arts Library, Dance Division. Special Collection. Hereafter referred to as **NYMG**.

4 From a newspaper interview in *Santa Barbara California News*, October 2, 1920. *Denishawn Scrapbooks*, **NYMG**.

5 Louise Levitas, "From Houri To Hurok: Pioneering Martha Graham Reaches Broadway Frontier," **NYMG**.

6 **BM**, 19.

7 "Modern Dancer," *Time*, March 9, 1936. **NYMG**. Other articles note that she was three years old.

8   Janet Mansfield Soares, *Louis Horst: Musician in a Dancer's World* (Durham, North Carolina: Duke University, 1992) 62. Hereafter referred to as **LH.**

9   Anna Kisselgoff, the dance critic for the *New York Times* frequently wrote about Martha Graham, and I have borrowed the consistent philosophies in describing Graham's work as "the thing itself."

10   **NYMG.**

11   "Martha Graham," **NYMG.**

12   **BM**, 48.

13   **PMC**, 87.

14   Robert Knott, "Paul Klee and the Mystic Center," in **TSI**, 133.

15   Ibid, 90-91.

16   Marian Horosko, *Martha Graham: The Evolution of Her Dance Theory and Training 1926-1991* (New York: a cappella, 1991) Hereafter referred to as **MGT.**

17   Nancy Wilson Ross, *The Notebooks of Martha Graham* (New York: Harcourt, Brace, Jovanovitch, 1973). Hereafter referred to as **TNOMG.**

18   **BM**, 274.

19   Selma Jean Cohen, Ed. *Dance as Theatre Art: Source Readings in Dance History from 1581 to the present. Princeton, N.J.: Princeton University Press, 1974*, second edition. "A Modern Dancer's Primer for Action" by Martha Graham, 135-142. Hereafter, **MDP.**

20   Mary Campbell, "An American Original," *Dance Magazine*, March 1999, 72.

21   **MGT**, 27.

22   Robert Tracy, *Goddess: Martha Graham's Dancers Remember* (New York: Limelight,1996), 25. From the words of former Graham dancer Betty MacDonald. Hereafter referred to as **MGDR.**

23   Toby Tobias, From "A Conversation with Martha Graham." *Dance Magazine*, March, 1984, 63. Hereafter, **CWMG.**

24   **CWMG**, 64.

25   **MGDR**, 171. Quote by former Graham dancer, Bertram Ross.

26   Sharamon Shalila, *The Chakra-Handbook* (Wilmot, Wisconsin: Lotus Light, 1991), 28.

27   **BM**, 46.

28   **NYMG.**

29   **NYMG.**

30   Dore Ashton, *Noguchi: East and West* (Berkeley: University of California, 1992), 263. Hereafter referred to as **NEW.**

31   Rosalyn L. Bruyere, Ed. *Wheels of Light* (New York: Simon and Schuster, 1994), 40.

32   Swami Kriyananda, *The Hindu Way of Awakening: Its Revelation, Its Symbols* (Nevada City, Calif.: Crystal Clarity, 1998), 201.

33   Agnes De Mille, *Martha* (New York: Vintage, 1991), 250. Hereafter, **MAR.**

34   **MDP.**

35   Thich Nhat Hanh, *Living Buddha, Living Christ* (New York: Riverhead, 1995), 15.

36 **MDP**.

37 Graham made many more dances which included the image of the Virgin Mary, however, I am concentrating on her early pieces specifically made to honor the Virgin Mary.

38 I am only referring to her Virgin Mary works, not the other later works with Virgin Mary themes.

39 The Proto Evangelium are considered the lost and hidden books of the Bible, and are not included in the New Testament and are part of the early Christian Apocrypha. They are not as respected in the United States as they are in Europe and in the realm of Eastern Orthodoxy. They include gospels, epistles, acts of various apostles, apocalypses, and homilies written in the early years of the church, from the second through the sixth centuries. They were used in the church before there was an official New Testament. The Christian Apocrypha contain narratives – many of which are not in the Bible – about Mary's parents, the lives of the Virgin and Joseph, and the activities of virtually all the apostles. Dating from about 150 to 200 C.E., the Proto-Gospel of James is likely the earliest of the apocryphal infancy gospels.

40 **TNOMG**, 275. Graham makes reference to a book called *Colour Symbolism*, page 139, but does not identify the author.

41 Retrieved January 24, 2001 at http://wesley.nnu.edu/noncanon/gospels/gosjames.htm. pg. 4-5.

42 Alexander Theroux, *Secondary Colors; Three Essays* (New York: Henry Holt & Company, 1996), 109.

43 S. J. Ousley, *Color Meditations: With Guide to Colour-Healing* (Essex: L.N. Fowler & Co. Ltd., 1949), 25.

44 **TNOMG**, 293.

45 Graham has scribbled a revelatory quote which addresses her identification with the gods. "Then the message of the great God fluttered in my breast & bade me prophesy." **TNOMG**, 291.

46 Rudolph Steiner, *Colour: Twelve Lectures by Rudolph Steiner* (London: Rudolph Steiner Press, 1992), 65. Hereafter referred to as **CRS**.

47 **MGT**, 34.

48 Don McDonagh, *Martha Graham: A Biography* (New York: Praeger, 1973), 58.

49 **BM.** 110.

50 **BM,** 113.

51 "Martha Graham on Dance," courtesy of the Jerome Robbins Dance Collection, Dance Clipping Files, New York City Performing Arts Library.

52 **NYMG**. *New York Times*, April 19, 1926. Ibid.

53 **MAR**, 83. Ruth St. Denis would later say that she appreciated Graham's talent but didn't think she had the right idea. Graham made up with St. Denis and later appeared at Jacob's Pillow with Ted Shawn in 1960.

54 Lincoln Kirstein, "Three Pamphlets Collected," (New York: Dance Horizons, 1967), 93.

55 **BM,** 114.

56 **CWMG,** 21.

57 **BM,** 200.

58 Ibid., 180.

59 **MAR,** 177.

60 **LH,** 63.

61 Ibid., 47.

62 **LH,** 113.

63 Ibid., 183.

64 Ibid., 183.

65 Ibid., 183-184.

66 Graham would later create *El Penitente* based on her interpretation of the Penitentes.

67 Susan Lamb, *Pueblo and Mission: Cultural Roots of the Southwest* (Flagstaff: Arizona: Northland, 1997), 74. Hereafter referred to as **PAM.**

68 **LH,** 89.

69 Ibid., 100.

70 John Martin, "The Dance: Miss Graham," *New York Times*, Feb. 8, 1931. **NYMG.**

71 John Martin, "The Dance: One Artist," *New York Times*, March 10, 1929. **NYMG.**

72 Mary Watkins, "The Work of Martha Graham Excels in Recent Dance Repertory Season," *New York Herald Tribune*, February 22, 1931. **NYMG.**

73 **NEW,** 61.

74 **MAR,** 177.

75 According to De Mille, before the performance Graham was in a frenzy about the costumes for the dancers and rushed off to Delancy Street to purchase dark-blue knit jersey for less than ten dollars. In the years since its premiere, the costumes have remained unchanged. Graham's dress was "a kind of organza which had an energy, a life, and an envelopment as if it were a cloud." **BM,** 53.

76 **MAR,** 178.

77 Ibid., 181.

78 Ibid., 179.

79 "Martha Graham: The Dancer Revealed," Kulture Films, 1994, WNET/NY. Hereafter referred to as **TDR.**

80 Ibid.

81 Ibid.

82 **MAR,** 191.

83 **NYMG.** No writer attributed.

84 **NYMG.** No writer attributed.

85 Mary Watkins. **NYMG.**

86 John Martin. **NYMG.**

87 Owen Dodson, *Martha Graham*, **NYMG.**

88 **NYMG.** Publication unknown.

Bibliography

Joan Accocella and Lynn Garafola. (Eds.) *Andre Levinson on Dance: Writings From Paris in the Twenties*. Hanover, New Hampshire: Wesleyan University Press, 1991.

Christy Adair. *Women and Dance: Sylphs and Sirens*. New York: New York University Press, 1992.

Doug Adams and Diane Apostolos-Cappadona, (Eds.) *Dance as Religious Studies*. New York: Crossroads, 1990.

Jack Anderson. *Ballet and Modern Dance*. Princeton, N.J.: Dance Horizons, 1992.

Leroy Appleton. *Symbolism in Liturgical Art*. New York: Charles Scribner, 1959.

Merle Armitage. *Martha Graham*. New York: Dance Horizons, 1966.

_____. *Martha Graham: The Early Years*. New York: Da Capo, 1978.

Geoffrey Ashe. *The Virgin*. London: Arkana, 1976.

Dore Ashton. *Noguchi East and West*. Berkeley: University of California Press, 1992.

St. Theresa of Avila. "Sudden Rapture." *Parabola*, Summer 1998, No.2.

Louis Bachman. *Religious Dances in the Christian Church and in Popular Medicine*. London: George Allen & Unwin Ltd. 1952.

Sally Banes. *Dancing Women: Female Bodies on Stage*. New York: Routledge, 1998.

Dorothy Bird. *Bird's Eye View: Dancing with Martha Graham*. Pittsburgh: University of Pittsburgh Press, 1997.

Joan Dexter Blackmer. *Acrobats of the Gods: Dance and Transformation*. Toronto: Inner City, 1989.

Frederika Blair. *Isadora: Portrait of the Artist as a Woman*. New York: McGraw Hill, 1986.

Bruno Borchert. *Mysticism: The History and Challenge*. New York: McGraw Hill, 1986.

Ann Braude. *Radical Spirits: Spiritualism and Women's Rights in 1900 America*. Boston, Massachusetts: Beacon, 1989.

Marcel Brion. *Kandinsky*. New York: Abrams, 1961.

Peter Brook. "Leaning on the Moment: A Conversation with Peter Brook," *Parabola*, Vol. IV. No.2, May 1979.

Raphael Brown. *The Life of the Virgin Mary As Seen by the Mystics*. Rockfors, Illinois: Tan, 1951.

Mary Campbell. "An American Original," *Dance Magazine*, March 1999.

Michael P. Carroll. *The Cult of the Virgin Mary: Psychological Origins*. Princeton, N.J.: Princeton University Press, 1986.

Hilda Charlton. *Divine Mother Speaks*. Woodstock: Golden Quest, 1993.

Nadia Choucha. *Surrealism and the Occult: Shamanism, Magic, Alchemy and the Birth of the Artistic Movement*. Rochester, Vermont: Destiny, 1991.

Anatole Chujoy. *The New York City Ballet*. New York: Knopf, 1953.

Constantine. "Ruth St. Denis and the Divine Dance," *Dance*, 1948.

Roger Copeland and Marshal Cohen. *What is Dance? Readings in Theory and Criticism*. New York: Oxford, 1983.

Ann Daly. *Done Into Dance: Isadora Duncan in America*. Bloomington & Indianapolis: Indiana University Press, 1995.

Agnes DeMille. Martha: *The Life and Work of Martha Graham*. New York: Vintage. 1992.

_____. "Martha Graham". From *The Atlantic*. Date Unknown.

Carla DeSola. *The Spirit Moves: Handbook of Dance and Prayer*. Austin, Texas: The Sharing Co., 1986.

Edward Dickson. *Poems of the Dance*. New York: Knopf, 1921.

Millicent Dillon. *After Egypt: Isadora Duncan and Mary Cassatt*. New York: Dutton, 1990.

Owen Dodson. "Martha Graham." Courtesy of Jerome Robbins Dance Collection, Dance Clipping Files, New York City Library for the Performing Arts.

J. Dominique. "Dance: Tribute to Miss Ruth." *Springfield Herald*, July 24, 1967.

Dore Duncan, et. all. *Isadora Duncan and Her World-Life Unto Art*. New York: Norton, 1993.

Irma Duncan. *Duncan Dancer*. Middletown, Conn.: Wesleyan University Press, 1966.

_____. "Personal Glimpses," *The Literary Digest*, October 8, 1927.

Isadora Duncan. *My Life*. New York: Boni and Liveright, 1927.

_____. *The Art of the Dance*. New York: Theater Arts Books, 1927.

_____. Clipping Files. Courtesy of Jerome Robbins Dance Collection, Dance Clipping Files, New York City Library for the Performing Arts.

_____. *Isadora Speaks*. San Francisco: City Lights, 1981.

Alexander Eliot. "The Third Hand," *Parabola*. Spring 1996, No.2.

Erte. *Erte: Things I Remember*. New York: Quadrangle, 1975.

George Ferguson. *Signs and Symbols in Christianity*. London: Oxford, 1954.

Suzanne Fincher. *Creating Mandalas*. Boston: Shambhala, 1991.

Carol Lee Flinders. *Enduring Grace*. San Francisco: Harper, 1993.

Hugh Ford. *The Left Bank Re-Visited*. University Park, Pennsylvania: The Pennsylvania State University Press, 1972.

Loie Fuller. *Goddess of Light*. Boston: Northeastern, 1997.

Sam Gill. "Focus." *Parabola*. Vol. IV. No. 2.

Albert Goldberg. "Ruth St. Denis: Prophet of the Dance, 85 and Still Kicking," *Los Angles Times*, Feb. 2, 1964.

Martha Graham. *The Notebooks of Martha Graham*. New York: Harcourt, Brace, Jovanovitch, 1973.

_____. *Blood Memory*. New York: Doubleday, 1991.

_____. Clipping Files. Courtesy of Jerome Robbins Dance Collection, Dance Clipping Files, New York City Library for the Performing Arts.

Andrew M. Greeley. *Ecstasy: A Way of Knowing*. Englewood Cliffs, New Jersey: Prentice Hall, 1974.

F.C. Happold. *Mysticism: A Study and an Anthology*. New York: Penguin, 1963.

Maurice Hamington. *Hail Mary? The Struggle for Ultimate Womanhood in Catholicism*. New York: Routledge, 1995.

Ernest Haskell. "The Matinee Girl Column," *The New York Dramatic Mirror*. May 9, 1903.

Corinne Heline. *Color and Music in the New Age*. La Canada, California: New Age, 1964.

Robert Henri. *The Art Spirit*. New York: Harper & Row, 1923.

Marian Horosko. *Martha Graham: The Evolution of Her Dance Theory and Training*. Chicago: Chicago Review, 1991.

Louis Horst. *Modern Dance Forms: In Relation to other Modern Arts*. Princeton, New Jersey: Dance Horizons, 1961.

Sisley Huddleston. *Paris Salons, Cafes, Studios: Being Social, Artistic and Literary Memories*. Philadelphia: Lippincott, 1928.

Doris Humphrey. *The Art of Making Dances*. New York: Grove, 1959.

William James. *The Varieties of Religious Experiences*. London: Longman's Green & Co., 1935.

Mrs. Jameson. *Legends of the Madonna As Represented in the Fine Arts*. Detroit: Omnigraphics, 1990, 1895.

Deborah Jowitt. *Time and the Dancing Image*. Berkeley: University of California Press, 1988.

Elizabeth Kendall. *Where She Dances*. New York: Knopf, 1979.

Francis King. (Ed.) *Ritual Magic and the Golden Dawn*. Rochester, Vermont: Destiny, 1987.

David Kingsley. *The Goddesses' Mirror*. New York: SUNY, 1989.

Lincoln Kirstein. *Lincoln Kirstein's Thirty Years: The New York City Ballet*. New York: Knopf, 1978.

_____. *Three Pamphlets Collected*. New York: Dance Horizons, 1967.

Susan Lamb. *Pueblo and Mission*. Arizona: Northland, 1997.

Lillian Lawler. *The Dance in Ancient Greece*. Middletown, Conn.: Wesleyan University Press, 1964.

Gerda Lerner. *The Creation of Feminist Consciousness*. New York: Oxford, 1993.

Julia Levien. *Duncan Dance*. New York: Horizons, 1994.

Kenneth C. Lindsay and Peter Vergo. *Kandinsky: Complete Writings on Art*. New York: DaCapo, 1994.

Lillian Lowenthal. *The Search for Isadora: The Legend and Legacy of Isadora Duncan*. Princeton, New Jersey: Dance Horizons, 1993

Glenn Loney. *Unsung Genius: The Passion of Dancer-Choreographer Jack Cole*. New York: Franklin Watts, 1984.

Mabel Dodge Luhan. *Movers and Shakers*. Albuquerque: University of New Mexico Press, 1936.

Allan Ross Mac-Dougal. *Isadora: A Revolutionary in Art and Love*. New York: Thomas Nelson, 1963.

Paul Magriel. *Isadora Duncan*. New York: Henry Holt, 1947.

_____. *Nijinsky, Pavolva, Duncan: Three Lives in Dance*. New York: DaCapo, 1947.

Caitlin Mathews. *The Elements of the Goddess*. London: Element, 1991.

_____. *Sophia*. London: Mandela, 1991.

Don McDonagh. *Martha Graham: A Biography*. New York: Praeger, 1973.

Karla McLaren. *Your Auras and Your Chakras; The Owner's Manual*. York Beach, Maine: Weiser, 1998.

Kamae Miller. *Wisdom Comes Dancing: Selected Writings of Ruth St. Denis in Dance, Spirituality and the Body*. Seattle, Washington: Peaceworks, 1997.

Shirley Nicholson. *The Goddess Re-Awakening*. London: Quest, 1989.

S.G. J. Ouseley. *Colour Meditations*. London: L.N. Fowler, 1949.

Isabelle M. Pagan. *From Pioneer to Poet: An Expansion of the Signs of the Zodiac Analyzed*. London: Theosophical Publishing, 1930.

Adolf Portman. *Colour Symbolism: Six Excerpts from the Eranos Yearbook, Eranos Series*. Dallas, Spring, 1977.

Kathleen Regnier. *The Spiritual Image in Modern Art*. London: Quest, 1987.

Janet Lynn Roseman, Ph.D. *Dance Masters: Interviews with Legends of Dance*. New York: Routledge, 2001.

Maria Schlinder. *Pure Color, Part 1*. London: New Culture, 1946.

Illya Ilyich Schneider. *The Russian Years*. New York: Harcourt Brace & World, 1968.

Victor Seroff. *The Real Isadora*. New York: Dial, 1971.

Sonu Shamdasi. (Ed.) *C.J. Jung: The Psychology of Kundalini Yoga*. Princeton: Bollingen, XCIX, 1996.

Sheila Sheramon and Bodo J. Baginski. *The Chakra-Handbook*. Wilmot, Wisc.: Lotus Light, 1991.

Ted Shawn. *1001 Nights*. New York: DaCapo, 1979.

Suzanne Shelton. *Divine Dancer*. New York: Doubleday, 1981.

Jane Sherman. *The Drama of a Denishawn Dancer*. Middletown: Wesleyan University Press, 1979.

Janet Mansfield Soares. *Louis Horst: Musician in a Dancer's World*. Durham, North Carolina: Duke University Press, 1992.

Rudolph Steiner. *Colour: Twelve Lectures by Rudolph Steiner*. London: Rudolph Steiner Press, 1996.

Frances Steegmuller. *Yours Isadora: The True Story of Isadora Duncan and Gordon Craig Told Through Their Letters and Diaries Never Published*. New York: Random House, 1974.

Iris Stewart. *Sacred Woman, Sacred Dance*. Rochester, Vermont: Inner Traditions, 2000.

Ruth St. Denis. *An Unfinished Life*. New York: Harper and Brothers, 1939.

_____. *Lotus Light*. Cambridge: The Riverside Press, 1932.

Bernard Taper. *Balanchine: A Biography*. Berkeley: University of California Press, 1984.

Karoun Tootikian. Phone Conversation in 1999. (Since deceased.)

Walter Terry. *The Dance Has Many Faces*. New York: Columbia University Press, 1966.

_____. *The More Living Life of Miss Ruth*. New York: Dodd Mead, 1969.

_____. *Isadora Duncan: Her Life, Her Art, Her Legacy*. New York: Dodd Mead, 1963.

Alexander Theroux. *The Primary Colors*. New York: Henry Holt, 1994.

_____. *The Secondary Colors*. New York: Henry Holt, 1996.

Robert Tracy. *Goddess: Martha Graham's Dancers Remember*. New York: Limelight, 1996.

Evelyn Underhill. *Practical Mysticism*. Columbus, Ohio: Ariel, 1914.

Geradus van der Leeuw. *Sacred and Profane Beauty: The Holy in Art*. David E. Green. (Trans.) New York: Holt, Rhinehart & Winston, 1963.

Rachel Vignier. *Gestures of Genius: Women, Dance and the Body*. Ontario: Mercury, 1994.

Marina Werner. *Alone of All Her Sex: The Myth and the Cult of the Virgin Mary*. New York: Vintage, 1983.

Nicholas Whitehead. *Patterns in Magical Christianity*. Albuquerque, New Mexico: Sun Chalice, 1996.

I am deeply grateful for the kindness and generosity of the following:

Alonzo King

Alonzo King is the Choreographer and Artistic Director of Alonzo King's LINES Ballet located in San Francisco, California. He is an internationally acclaimed choreographer with works in the repertories of over fifty companies including: Frankfurt Ballet, Joffrey Ballet, Dance Theater of Harlem, Alvin Ailey American Dance Theater, Hong Kong Ballet, North Carolina Dance Theater and Washington Ballet. He has worked extensively in opera, television and film and has choreographed works for prima ballerina Natalia Makarova and film star Patrick Swayze. Renowned for his skill as a teacher, Mr. King has been guest Ballet Master for many dance companies including: National Ballet of Canada, Les Ballets de Monte Carlo, San Francisco Ballet, Ballet Rambert, and Ballet West.

In 1982, he founded Alonzo King's LINES Ballet, which has developed into an international touring company. He has collaborated with legendary musicians including Pharoah Sanders, Zakir Hussein, Bernice Johnson Reagan, Nubian Oud, Master Hamza al Din, and Pavel Syzmanski. In 1989, Alonzo King founded the San Francisco Dance Center, one of the largest dance facilities on the West Coast, replete with the LINES Ballet School and the Pre-Professional Program.

Mr. King is the recipient of the NEA Choreographer's Fellowship and the National Dance Residency Program. He has received four Isadora Duncan Awards, the Hero Award from the Union Bank, and the Excellence Award from KGO-TV in San Francisco. He has served on the panels for the National Endowment of the Arts, California Arts Council, City of Columbus Arts Council, and Lila-Wallace-Reader's Digest Arts Partners Program. He is the former Commissioner for the city and county of San Francisco, and a noted writer and lecturer on the art of dance. Contact: Alonzo King's LINES Ballet; www.linesballet.org; 26 7th Street, San Francisco, California, 94103.

Norton Owen

Norton Owen is the Director of Preservation at Jacob's Pillow Dance Festival. The mission of Jacob's Pillow Dance Festival, founded by dancer Ted Shawn, is to support dance creation, presentation, education, and preservation; and to engage and deepen public appreciation and support for dance. Contact: Jacob's Pillow Dance Festival, Box 287, Lee, Massachusetts, 01238. Phone: 413.327.1234. See: www. jacobspillow.org.

Jan Gardner-Broske

Jan Gardner-Broske is the Curator of the University Museums, University of Delaware. Contact: www.museums.udel. edu. University of Delaware, 114 Old College, Newark, Delaware. 19716-2509. Phone: 302.831.8242.

Scott Hess

Scott Hess is a commercial and arts photographer working in the San Francisco Bay area. His work covers a wide spectrum from nature, to current social and artistic movements, to images reflecting our global spiritual culture. Examples of his work may be seen at: www.scotthessphoto .com.

Iris J. Stewart

Iris J. Stewart is the author of *Sacred Woman, Sacred Dance: Awakening Spirituality Through Movement and Ritual,* published by Inner Traditions. This unique book explores the history of women's ways of expressing the Divine. See: www. SacredDancer.com. Email: Iris@SacredDancer. com.

Marriott Library's Manuscript Division at the University of Utah.

The Manuscripts Division at the Marriott Library houses over 2,000 collections of original, unpublished materials. Diaries, correspondence, artwork, histories, essays, autobiographies, and many other materials are available. Contact: University of Utah, Marriott Library, 295 S. 1500 E. Salt Lake City, Utah. 84112-0860.

Jane Grossenbacher

Jane Grossenbacher, photographer. "My favorite adventures as a photographer is to travel to foreign lands and be lost (one day at a time) and witness, as a true outsider, what unfolds. Spontaneous experiences have been a theme in my images for many years. Black and white provides the simple, complicated, and mysterious at the same moment – the essential elements of spontaneity." Contact: www.babbazulu.com. Jane Grossenbacher, 499 Alabama Street, #129. San Francisco, California 94110. Phone: 415.863.1651.

Lori Belilove

Lori Belilove, Founder and Artistic Director of the Isadora Dance Foundation studied with the first and second generation Duncan dancers (or "Isadorables") and is one of the world's foremost interpreters of the Duncan technique. She is the living embodiment of Isadora's mastery of weight and form, and has dedicated her life to the preservation and promotion of Isadora's genius.

The Isadora Duncan Dance Foundation

The Isadora Duncan Dance Foundation was founded in 1979 as a non-profit center dedicated to keeping the dances of Isadora Duncan alive with a school, performing troupe, and historical archive. The mission is to extend the dream, dance, and indomitable spirit of Isadora Duncan to generations to come through original choreography, educational workshops and programs that nurture the soul and lift the spirit. Contact: www.isadoraduncan.org; The Isadora Duncan Dance Foundation, 141 W. 26th Street, 3rd Floor, New York, New York 10001-6800. Phone: 212.691.5040.

The Ruth St. Denis Foundation

The Ruth St. Denis Foundation was founded by Ruth St. Denis in 1948 for the preservation of the creative works of Ruth St. Denis. The archive holdings include the choreography, photography, film, video, costumes, papers, writings and intellectual property in regards to the spiritual emphasis of divine dance and spiritual arts. For twenty years, Karoun Tootikian worked with St. Denis as the head of the school and the company; The Ruth St. Denis Concert Dancers. Together they documented the last official version of the St. Denis repertory. Following St. Denis's death, Tootikian furthered the company, school and foundation, including a European tour, video archives and international teaching until her death. The Ruth St. Denis Foundation continues under the direction of Dr. Adrian Ravarour, President. Wendy Uyeda is the head of The Ruth St. Denis Concert Dancers, and Virginia Cotton is the Director of the Ruth St. Denis School. Contact:ruthstdenis@yahoo.com; The Ruth St. Denis Foundation, PO Box 39823 Los Angeles, California 90039.

Kelly Borsheim

Kelly Borsheim, artist. "I am interested in the more personal moments of our lives. I am also fascinated by the duality of nature, especially the idea that two opposing concepts exist in a strange kind of balance. I find that creating works of art in bronze and stone offers me another way to explore coexisting opposites. For example, I like a soft curve in a hard material. I love it when people are drawn to one of my works and reach out to touch it, since touch is the most intimate and universal sense we have." www.borsheimarts.com. Borsheim Arts Studio, P.O. Box 340, Cedar Creek, Texas 78612. Phone: 512.303.3929.
Email: sculptor@borsheimarts.com

Kim Goldfarb

Kim Goldbarb, artist. "'Ritual Dancer' was inspired by a perfectly shaped piece of driftwood found on Vancouver Island, B.C. Her torso and legs were formed from this one piece of wood. Head, arms, feet and hands were added from other pieces of found wood and clay. I felt her serene pose was fitting of the dancer after her performance. Dance can be like meditation, helping one enter an altered state of consciousness. 'Ritual Dancer' speaks to us of exotic cultures

where dance and ritual mark rites of passage."
Email: wrightpub@comcast.net

Mark Roseman

Mark Roseman is the Deputy Director for Child Access for the National Children's Rights Council. Since 1985, the Children's Rights Council has provided research and educational programs to strengthen parent-child relationships following parental separations and divorce. Mr. Roseman is a divorce educator and consultant. He is known for his work photographing nature, and nautical landscapes. Contact: www.gocrc.com; or Libros3@ aol.com.

The Dances of Universal Peace

The Dances of Universal Peace were brought together in the late 1960's by Samuel L. Lewis, a Sufi Murshid (teacher) and Rinzai Zen Master, who also studied deeply in the mystical traditions. Lewis was deeply influenced by his contact and spiritual apprenticeship with Hazrat Inayat Khan, and by Ruth St. Denis. PeaceWorks serves as a coordinating nexus for the worldwide dances. Contact: PeaceWorks International Network for the Dances of Universal Peace; www.dancesofuniversalpeace.org; INOFFICE@dancesofuniversalpeace.org; P.O. Box 55994, Seattle, Washington, 98155-0994.

Martha Graham Resources

A division of the Martha Graham Center of Contemporary Dance, Martha Graham Resources was created in 2002 to preserve, restore, interpret, and share the assets of one of the world's most extensive collections in dance history: sets, costumes, audio and video recordings, photographs and correspondence. This department licenses the use of resources owned by the Martha Graham Center to enable other institutions to mount productions of the dances of Martha Graham, further develop the Center's archives, and create new artistic programs. www.marthagrahamdance.org.

Index

WOMEN CALLED TO THE PATH OF RUMI
The Way of the Whirling Dervish
by Shakina Reinhertz

This book shares the experience of Turning practice by women of the Mevlevi Order of Whirling Dervishes. The beauty and mystery of the Whirling Dervishes have captured the mythic imagination of the Western world for centuries. Rumi, the great Sufi saint of 13th-century Turkey, taught both male and female students this whirling dance, but in the centuries after his death women were excluded from participation. Not until the late 1970s, when Shaikh Suleyman Dede brought the turn ritual to America, was this practice again opened to women. The heart of the book is the personal experience of contemporary women – interviews with over two dozen American initiates (from adolescents to wise elders), many of whom have practiced on this path for twenty years or more.

"I love the wisdom and fire of this book. It's full of the light of longing and people trying to experience the mystery of that truth."

– Coleman Barks, translator of Rumi's poetry.

Paper, 300 pages, 200 black and white photos and illustrations, $23.95 ISBN: 1-890772-04-6

THE WOMAN AWAKE
Feminine Wisdom for Spiritual Life
by Regina Sara Ryan

Through the stories and insights of great women whom the author has met or been guided by in her own journey, this book highlights many faces of the Divine Feminine: the silence, the solitude, the service, the power, the compassion, the art, the darkness, the sexuality. Read about: the Sufi poetess Rabia (8th century) and contemporary Sufi master Irina Tweedie; Hildegard of Bingen, author Kathryn Hulme (*The Nun's Story*), German healer and mystic Dina Rees, and others. Includes personal interviews with contemplative Christian monk Mother Tessa Bielecki, artist Meinrad Craighead, and Zen roshi and anthropologist Joan Halifax.

Paper, 20+ photos, 518 pages, $19.95   ISBN: 0-934252-79-3

TO ORDER: Use accompanying order form, or call 800-381-2700, or visit our website at www.hohmpress.com

AS IT IS
A Year on the Road with a Tantric Teacher
by M. Young

A first-hand account of a one-year journey around the world in the company of *tantric* teacher Lee Lozowick. This book catalogues the trials and wonders of day-to-day interactions between a teacher and his students, and presents a broad range of his teachings given in seminars from San Francisco, California to Rishikesh, India. *As It Is* considers the core principles of *tantra*, including non-duality, compassion (the Bodhisattva ideal), service to others, and transformation within daily life. Written as a narrative, this captivating book will appeal to practitioners of *any* spiritual path. Readers interested in a life of clarity, genuine creativity, wisdom and harmony will find this an invaluable resource.

Paper, 840 pages, 24 b&w photos, $29.95   ISBN: 0-934252-99-8

THE YOGA TRADITION:
Its History, Literature, Philosophy and Practice
by Georg Feuerstein, Ph.D.   Foreword by Ken Wilber

A complete overview of the great Yogic traditions of: Raja-Yoga, Hatha-Yoga, Jnana-Yoga, Bhakti-Yoga, Karma-Yoga, Tantra-Yoga, Kundalini-Yoga, Mantra-Yoga and many other lesser known forms. Includes translations of over twenty famous Yoga treatises, like the *Yoga-Sutra* of Patanjali, and a first-time translation of the *Goraksha Paddhati*, an ancient Hatha Yoga text. Covers all aspects of Hindu, Buddhist, Jaina and Sikh Yoga. A necessary resource for all students and scholars of Yoga.

"No more adept or comprehensive study of yoga aimed at a Western audience is to be found."   – American Library Association, *BOOKLIST*

Paper, 540 pages, over 200 illustrations, $29.95   ISBN: 1-890772-18-6

TO ORDER: Use accompanying order form, or call 800-381-2700, or visit our website at www.hohmpress.com

THE JUMP INTO LIFE:
Moving Beyond Fear
by Arnaud Desjardins   Foreword by Richard Moss, M.D.

"Say *Yes* to life," the author continually invites in this welcome guidebook to the spiritual path. For anyone who has ever felt oppressed by the life-negative seriousness of religion, this book is a timely antidote. In language that translates the complex to the obvious, Desjardins applies his simple teaching of happiness and gratitude to a broad range of weighty topics, including sexuality and intimate relationships, structuring an "inner life," the relief of suffering, and overcoming fear.

Paper, 278 pages, $12.95   ISBN: 0-934252-42-4

HALFWAY UP THE MOUNTAIN
The Error of Premature Claims to Enlightenment
by Mariana Caplan   Foreword by Fleet Maull

Dozens of first-hand interviews with students, respected spiritual teachers and masters, together with broad research are synthesized here to assist readers in avoiding the pitfalls of the spiritual path. Topics include: mistaking mystical experience for enlightenment; ego inflation, power and corruption among spiritual leaders; the question of the need for a teacher; disillusionment on the path…and much more.

"Caplan's illuminating book…urges seekers to pay the price of traveling the hard road to true enlightenment."
                                        – *Publisher's Weekly*

Paper, 600 pages, $21.95   ISBN: 0-934252-91-2

TO ORDER: Use accompanying order form, or call 800-381-2700, or visit our website at www.hohmpress.com

THE ALCHEMY OF LOVE AND SEX
by Lee Lozowick   Foreword by Georg Feuerstein, Ph.D.

Reveals 70 "secrets" about love, sex and relationships. Lozowick recognizes the immense conflict and confusion surrounding love, sex, and tantric spiritual practice. Advocating neither asceticism nor hedonism, he presents a middle path—one grounded in the appreciation of simple human relatedness. Topics include:* what men want from women in sex, and what women want from men * the development of a passionate love affair with life * how to balance the essential masculine and essential feminine * the dangers and possibilities of sexual Tantra * the reality of a genuine, sacred marriage. . .and much more.

"...attacks Western sexuality with a vengeance." – *Library Journal*

Paper, 312 pages, $16.95   ISBN: 0-934252-58-0

JOURNEY
From Political Activism to the Work
by Janet Rose

This book recounts the story of a spiritual journey that led the author from a life of political and social activism to a life of spiritual transformation. Having worked as a newspaper reporter, a manager of a food cooperative, a coordinator of a rural health service and a VISTA volunteer, Janet Rose thought her next step was to build her practice as a psychotherapist in a large southeastern city. In the summer of 1986, however, almost overnight her life took a radical turn. Following inner mystical guidance, she turned west, to the mountains of Colorado, to "find God more deeply." In her quest for genuine wisdom, compassion and service, she left behind the vestiges of her previous life to pursue a path of renunciation and to apprentice herself to a spiritual teacher. How that choice was made, what that commitment entailed, and how it has changed every aspect of her life is what this book is about.

Paper, 384 pages, $19.95   ISBN: 1-890772-04-6

MARROW OF FLAME:
Poems of the Spiritual Journey
by Dorothy Walters   Foreword by Andrew Harvey

This compilation of 105 new poems documents and celebrates the author's interior journey of *kundalini* awakening. Her poems cut through the boundaries of religious provincialism to the essence of longing, love and union that supports every authentic spiritual tradition, as she writes of the Mother Goddess, as well as of Krishna, Rumi, Bodhidharma, Hildegard of Bingen, and many others. Best-selling spiritual author and poet Andrew Harvey has written the book's Introduction. His commentary illuminates aspects of Dorothy's spiritual life and highlights the "unfailing craft" of her poems.

"Dorothy Walters writes poetry that speaks to us from the heart to the heart, gently touching our deepest spiritual stirrings."

– Riane Eisler, author, *The Chalice and the Blade.*

Paper, 144 pages, $12.00   ISBN: 0-934252-96-3

RUMI, THIEF OF SLEEP
180 Quatrains from the Persian
Translations by Shahram Shiva   Foreword by Deepak Chopra

This book contains 180 translations of Rumi's short devotional poems, or *quatrains*. Shiva's versions are based on his own carefully documented translation from the Farsi (Persian), the language in which Rumi wrote.

"In *Thief Of Sleep*, Shahram Shiva (who embodies the culture, the wisdom and the history of Sufism in his very genes) brings us the healing experience. I recommend his book to anyone who wishes *to remember*. This book will help you do that."– Deepak Chopra, author of *How to Know God*

Paper, 120 pages, $11.95   ISBN: 1-890772-05-4

RETAIL ORDER FORM FOR HOHM PRESS BOOKS

Name _____ Phone ( ) _____

Street Address or P.O. Box _____

City _____ State _____ Zip Code _____

QTY	TITLE	ITEM PRICE	TOTALPRICE
	WOMEN CALLED TO THE PATH OF RUMI	$23.95	
	THE WOMAN AWAKE	$19.95	
	AS IT IS	$29.95	
	THE YOGA TRADITION	$29.95	
	THE JUMP INTO LIFE	$12.95	
	HALFWAY UP THE MOUNTAIN	$21.95	
	THE ALCHEMY OF LOVE AND SEX	$16.95	
	JOURNEY	$19.95	
	MARROW OF FLAME	$12.00	
	RUMI — THIEF OF SLEEP	$11.95	

SURFACE SHIPPING CHARGES:
1st book $5.00
Each additional item ....add $1.00

SHIP MY ORDER:
☐ Surface U.S. Mail—Priority   ☐ Fex-Ex Ground (Mail + $3.00)
☐ 2nd Day Air (Mail + $5.00)   ☐ Next Day Air (Mail + $15.00)

SUBTOTAL:

SHIPPING:
(see right)

TOTAL:

METHOD OF PAYMENT:
☐ Check or M.O.   Payable to Hohm Press, P.O. Box 2501, Prescott, AZ 86302
☐ Call 1-800-381-2700 to place your credit card order
☐ Or call 1-928-717-1779 to fax your credit card order
☐ Information for Visa/MasterCard/American Express order only:

Card#_____-_____-_____-_____ Expiration Date:_____

Visit our Website to view our complete catalog: www.hohmpress.com
ORDER NOW! Call 1-800-381-2700 or fax your order to 1-928-717-1779
(Remember to include your credit card information.)

About the Author

Dr. Janet Lynn Roseman is a dance scholar, teacher, and critic. She is a Clinical Instructor in the Family Medicine Department at Brown University Medical School and is committed to elevating the sacred aspects of medicine. She currently works with people with cancer using spectra-immunology, a non-invasive form of color and light therapy. She can be reached at Dancejan@aol.com.